W9-CCX-784

Women Doing Excellently

Paula Clifford is Writer and Co-publications Manager in the Churches Team at Christian Aid.

She has written scripts for BBC Radio and has published a number of books. She lives in Oxford.

Other publications by the author include

A Brief History of End Time (Lion)

The Servant King (Christian Aid)

New Dictionary of Christian Ethics and
Pastoral Theology (contributor – IVP)

Women Doing Excellently

*Biblical women
and their successors*

Paula Clifford

'Many women have done excellently, but you
surpass them all.'
Proverbs 31:29

CANTERBURY
PRESS
Norwich

'While the light lasts I shall not forget, and in the darkness I shall remember.'

– W. S. Landor

First published in 2001 by The Canterbury Press Norwich
(a publishing imprint of Hymns Ancient & Modern Limited
a registered charity)
St Mary's Works, St Mary's Plain
Norwich, Norfolk, NR3 3BH

British Library Cataloguing in Publication Data

A catalogue record of this book is available
from the British Library

ISBN 1-85311-404-9

Typeset by Rowland Phototypesetting Ltd,
Bury St Edmunds, Suffolk
Printed and bound in Great Britain by
Bookmarque Ltd, Croydon, Surrey

Contents

Introduction

At first glance biblical women may seem to be few and far between. In a society which we know to have been patriarchal and, some would have us believe, deliberately repressive of women, what scope might there be for women to reveal and use their gifts other than in their traditional roles as wives and mothers?

The answer then may seem surprising. One has only to look closely at the books of the Old Testament, supposedly produced by men for men, to find some of the most outstanding women of ancient history. There are leaders and thinkers, prophets and poets. Some are thrust to the front of the stage by their oratorical skills, others remain silently and effectively active in the background. There are women coping on their own, while others face the challenges of large families or the stigma of childlessness.

If the Old Testament is rich in its portrayal of a wide variety of women, the New Testament is notable for just a few outstanding characters. We know that the ministry of Jesus was marked by a respect for women, whatever their status in life, and that there were women who faithfully followed him alongside the male disciples, even to Calvary. The new role accorded to women is evident at every stage in Jesus' life, from his birth to the young Mary, acclaimed by the prophetess Anna, through his healing miracles, many of them involving women, to the cross, where women remain silently faithful, and resurrection, where women are the first witnesses to the risen Lord. In the New Testament church, though, few women are mentioned by name, but they are certainly present, even though the action is dominated by Paul and Peter and their associates in the unfolding drama of the founding of the new religion.

What I find fascinating is that the gifts and distinguishing characteristics of these biblical women are echoed and developed by women down the centuries. Although many of those I have chosen to write about would probably have been aghast to think that someone was comparing them to the illustrious and holy women of Scripture, the fact remains that their speaking and leading abilities, their resilience and their faithful service of one another and of God are there to be seen throughout Christian history.

The way in which I have grouped biblical women and their successors is one which I have found helpful and convenient, but every reader will have a view as to how it could be done differently. Real people, unlike the creations of literary writers, do not fall neatly into such categories. Some of the women I have labelled outstanding for the actions they have taken might equally well be distinctive for speaking out, or indeed could fall into a different grouping, which I have not used, of women of courage.

The women I have focused on as successors to women in the Bible are equally a matter of personal choice. Other people will have their own ideas, and, given the immense contribution of women to history, religion, society and culture, it is only right that they should. And always present at the back of one's mind are all those women who are worthy successors to the biblical characters, but whose qualities and skills will never be acknowledged outside their own immediate circle.

I have also restricted my choice to Christian women, including among them Simone Weil, whose faith was deeply Christian although she was never formally received into the church. This has of course led to some significant omissions, particularly of women of other faiths. It has saddened me to have to leave out one such outstanding woman of our time, the Burmese leader Aung San Suu Kyi. Others would no doubt want to include Mrs Indira Gandhi or some of the great nineteenth-century non-Christian reformers. Whether or not they would acknowledge it, these women too have much in common with biblical women, and may also be classed as excellent.

I have never considered myself to be a feminist, of either the 'old' or 'new' variety. But over the years I have come to value deeply and to respect all that women are and have the potential to be in every aspect of modern life, and I would passionately defend their right to be where their gifts and inclinations lead them. So perhaps I am a feminist after all.

Finally, I would like to pay tribute to the many women among whom I have lived, worked and ministered, who have helped my thinking, supported and challenged me. To them I am grateful and hope that they will enjoy meeting the women I have selected here.

Oxford, Spring 2001

I

Women Speaking Out

The women who went to Jesus' tomb on the first Easter morning were not, as far as we know, naturally gifted speakers, and we know more about what they felt than what they said. Grief-stricken and exhausted after the events of the previous week, when they were confronted by an angel and an empty tomb they were quite simply terrified. The form of the earliest account of these events in Mark's Gospel ends abruptly with the words 'they said nothing to anyone, for they were afraid', although later versions modify this by including the joy that was mixed with the fear and the detail that the women passed the news on.

These women – two of them in Matthew's Gospel, three in Mark – who were entrusted with the most significant message of all time, had not until then been great communicators. They were thrust into a unique situation and had no option but to respond by speaking out, passing on the news. Medieval commentators used to argue that God chose women to spread the news of Christ's resurrection because he knew that they would not be able to keep quiet about it. This observation would of course be seen nowadays as patronizing, reinforcing an unacceptable stereotype, even though some modern-day evangelists still like to refer to women 'gossiping the gospel'. What is more important is that the women who witnessed the resurrection were there because of their conventional role in society at the time. It fell to them to go and anoint properly with spices the body which had been buried with almost unseemly haste before the Passover; and in carrying out that task, the women found themselves in this terrifying situation, which laid on them the irresistible demand that they should go and tell the world.

Where women in the Bible, and women subsequently in history, are presented in this role of speaking out, this is one likely scenario – they are there at the time and have no option but to talk about it. There are, though, other possible sets of circumstances. One is that women are led to speak because they have a certain influence in a given situation: they may not have power to act themselves, but are close to those who can, as was the case with Esther; or they may be in a position to comment on the actions of another person because of a relationship of friendship or kinship, as Miriam did. Alternatively, they may have a wider influence in society and speak out because what they say matters and will lead other people to take action. Then there are the women who have particular gifts of communication, whether this is the gift of prophecy, relaying God's will to others, or a gift of speaking which goes hand in hand with their intellectual activities – women who nowadays are likely to be found among academics, politicians, theologians, writers or broadcasters. The oldest biblical model of such a person is to be found in the Book of Judges, and she was herself a judge: a good starting point for looking at women who are called to speak.

Deborah the Judge (Judges 4 and 5)

'Awake, awake, Deborah! . . . utter a song!' (Judges 5:12)

The story of Deborah has come down to us through over 3,000 years of history, and it is, quite simply, a success story. Deborah's career took her into politics, the law and religion, and she seems to have excelled in all of them. In order to do that she had certain gifts, of which wisdom and discernment and the power to communicate these would have been well to the fore.

In the history of Israel, the period of the judges was the time when the tribes of Israel were united under a series of short-term charismatic leaders, before becoming a nation proper under a monarchy. The judges were raised up by God to lead Israel in times of crisis, when the people had brought difficulties on themselves through their disobedience to God. In order to 'deliver' the people from their troubles these judges were given temporary authority, which generally involved military action as well as spiritual leadership.

Among these leaders, who would by definition have been gifted and God-fearing, Deborah was outstanding. Not only is she the only woman judge on record, but she had the title 'Mother in Israel' (Judges 5:7), which, in the words of a German theologian, 'as regards religious authority places her on a par with the priest'.[1] And although she lived a long time ago and had a distinctive task at a particular moment in history, Deborah's gifts, and especially her use of them, have found their echo in the lives of women in very different cultures down the ages.

Deborah was not only a judge in this sense of one of a line of leaders of Israel, among whom Gideon and Samuel are probably the best known. She was also a judge in the legal sense, and a particularly gifted one at that. She judged Israel (Judges 4:4), which meant that Israelites came to her if they could not get satisfaction from their own local judges or if there were inter-tribal disputes to be settled. The ability to use words well would have been a crucial tool of her legal trade. Deborah's call to leadership, following the pattern of God's call to other judges, was the result of the people's cry to God for help at a time of oppression and danger (4:2–3). The military task ahead of her seems to have been unusually daunting, even though the writer may have exaggerated the strength of the opposition: she was to confront the might of 900 chariots of iron, which would have been covered with iron as well as having iron weapons. Deborah's plan was to disable this force by mounting an ambush. And her special qualities as a woman called to speak out emerge both in the way in which she handled her plan and in her relationship to her assistant Barak.

An immediately striking feature of the way Deborah behaves in formulating her military strategy is that she speaks with an authority that is God-given. She summons Barak to hear the orders which she has for him under God; she is confident ('I will give [the enemy] into your hand') but she respects Barak's right to know what is going on, explaining her own role in the action so that Barak can fully understand her plan. Deborah is also open to discussion, agreeing to Barak's suggestion that she should accompany him, but is conscious at once of the consequences: that she and not Barak will be regarded as the victor. And this reveals other aspects of Deborah as a speaker: she is quick-thinking and forthright, there is no beating about the bush. Barak has to see straightaway that if he persists in his argument – which may well have been based on understandable caution – he will not get the credit; it will go to Deborah, a woman, instead. If Deborah is offering Barak a chance to change his mind it is a generous gesture, but once the decision is taken it is immediately put into effect.

It is possible that there is a further contrast between Deborah and Barak which is missing from the standard biblical translations. The Septuagint (the Greek translation of the Old Testament) has an addition to Judges 4:8 in which Barak acknowledges Deborah's spiritual authority and his own lack of religious insight, saying 'I do not in fact know the day when God will lead me, with his angel at my side.' So Barak accepts Deborah's spiritual and military authority and summons his own considerable military resources of 10,000 men.

Deborah is equally assured in her speech when it is time to fight, and again she displays a confidence which stems from her trust in God: 'Up! For this is the day in which the Lord has given Sisera into your hand. The Lord is indeed going out before you' (4:14). In the battle the focus of the action shifts from Deborah to Barak, although, as Deborah has already made clear, behind it all is God: 'The Lord threw Sisera and all his chariots into a panic before Barak' (4:15).

Judges 5, which essentially recounts the same events as the previous chapter but in the form of a poem sung by Deborah, reinforces Deborah's qualities in leadership which emerge from Judges 4. It also gives her a further role in creating a hymn of praise to God which records his powerful intervention in this episode in Israel's history and includes details of her own leadership, her trust in God and the people's willingness to follow suit.

Having used her confident and forthright speaking abilities to lead her people out to fight, Deborah is now seen as more reflective, ordering events and setting the military conflict in a theological framework. So her poem opens and closes in praise to God. Then God is shown as active in battle, and the natural world seems to join with him: the stars fight against Sisera (5:20) and the rushing torrent of Kishon sweeps Sisera's army away (5:21). Finally there is the sad detail of Sisera's mother waiting for the son who will never return (5:28–30). The manner of Sisera's death at the hands of Jael is not relevant to the story of Deborah and may belong to a different tradition.

But some commentators have suggested that the sympathetic treatment of Sisera's mother indicates female authorship, although it has to be asked whether they would say the same thing if the song had been anonymous.

Deborah, then, is a woman with a special gift of wise and forthright speech, which she uses in the service of God and of her fellow Israelites. She speaks out with a confidence born of knowing that what she has to say comes from God. Yet this does not lead her to turn a deaf ear to those under her, and she is, further, attributed with the task of recording the events in which she has been the key player and reflecting God's central and guiding role in the whole episode.

Even so, despite Deborah's unassailable role of leadership the name of Barak comes to be cited more than hers. In 1 Samuel 12:11 it is Barak not Deborah who is included among four people described as sent by God to deliver the people from their enemies, and the writer to the Hebrews lists him among those who 'through faith . . . became mighty in war, put foreign armies to flight' (Hebrews 11:33, 34). But there are no biblical grounds at all for asserting, as David Watson did, that 'Deborah . . . took the lead in the absence of strong male leadership'.[2] Rather, Deborah spoke out using her God-given gifts and as 'Mother in Israel' achieved success for herself and, more importantly, for the whole people of God.

Influence in the Family: Miriam and Esther

Miriam the Leader's Sister (Numbers 11, 12)

Miriam, the prophetess and sister of Aaron (Exodus 15:20) was also, according to tradition, sister to Moses, so she was ideally placed to tackle Moses if there was discontent among the people. Numbers 12 recounts how she and

Aaron first rebuked Moses for his marriage to a Cushite (possibly just an excuse for an argument) and then expressed their grievance at the suggestion that God would speak only through Moses. This incurs God's displeasure, and Miriam is briefly struck with leprosy as punishment.

This is an incident which needs to be seen in a wider context to appreciate the significance of Miriam's forthright speech to her brother. Numbers 11 tells of Moses' appointment of seventy elders who also received the spirit of prophecy. This obviously inspired some jealousy and the feeling on the part of some people that only Moses should prophesy, although Moses himself condemns this attitude. It is against this background that Miriam uses her family position to make her complaint, which enables the matter to be brought out into the open and for God to deal with it once and for all.

Miriam, whose forthrightness is comparable to Deborah's, although she lacks Deborah's wisdom, is a very different character from Moses, who is described as the meekest of men. Clearly he never claimed any special privileges for himself. Along with Aaron Miriam is summoned into the Lord's presence (12:5), and is told of the basic difference between prophets like herself, to whom God appears in dreams or visions, and Moses who 'beholds the form of the Lord' (12:8) and is addressed directly rather than in dreams. The importance of this can be inferred from God's anger at Miriam's speech and the leprosy he inflicts on her. It is only thanks to Aaron's plea to Moses, in which Aaron willingly shares the blame, and Moses' heartfelt plea to God that the punishment is lifted. It is replaced by seven days' isolation, suggesting that the leprosy in fact disappeared immediately, as custom demanded that the victim be isolated for a week to be sure that the condition was cured.

Miriam's outburst may have been damaging in the short

term, but it seems to have had the effect of putting an end to the squabbles about who should prophesy, and it established Moses' supremacy in a way which perhaps would not have been possible if it had been left to him. No lasting blame attached to either Miriam or Aaron (who suffered no punishment at all) and their separate deaths are recorded in Numbers 20, along with the detail that Aaron was mourned for thirty days.

Esther: Wife of a Persian King (The Book of Esther)

If Miriam's outspokenness to her brother ultimately resolved a question of God-given authority, Esther's decision to speak out, very much later in Jewish history, served God's purposes only indirectly. Esther's task was to save her people from mass slaughter in the Persian capital Susa, at no little risk to herself. Yet Jewish solidarity has always been closely bound up with religious belief, and while the Book of Esther tends to be regarded as historical fiction, the person of Esther is an interesting addition to the list of biblical women who are compelled by circumstance to speak out.

King Ahasuerus chose to marry Esther for her beauty, knowing nothing of her Jewish background. After the marriage, Esther's cousin Mordecai, who had brought her up as his adopted daughter, found himself in trouble for refusing to bow down before Haman, the king's favourite, whom the writer goes on to reveal as the enemy of the Jews. At Haman's instigation, the king gives orders to 'destroy the Jewish people on a given day . . . and to plunder their goods' (3:13). At that point Mordecai appeals to Esther, who at first claims she can do nothing, because she may not approach the king, on pain of death, without first being summoned by him.

It is then that the Book of Esther makes its one reference

to God, and only in very veiled terms, yet Mordecai's speech is sufficient to convince Esther to speak out, despite her personal danger:

> For if you keep quiet at such a time as this, help and protection will come to the Jews from another quarter [i.e. from God], but you and your father's family will perish. Yet, who knows whether it was not for such a time as this that you were made queen? (4:14)

The suggestion that Esther may be where she is to serve God's purpose, and the hint of God's wrath if she fails, is enough to cause her to brave the danger and speak out, to use her influence with her husband for the sake of her people.

The situation is complicated by Haman's hatred for Mordecai and his plot against him. So when Esther approaches her husband she speaks first in a roundabout way, inviting him to a meal: 'My petition and request is: If I have found favour in the sight of the king, let the king and Haman come to the dinner that I shall prepare them' (5:8). Only on the second day of feasting does Esther explain what she really wants – for her own and her people's lives to be spared – while all the time clothing her request in loving and respectful language (7:4). The king responds by having the plotter Haman executed, but there is still the matter of the decree to exterminate the Jews. This is when Esther reveals her full emotion, falling at her husband's feet in tears (8:3), yet telling him exactly what she wants him to do, before ending on a note of personal despair: 'How can I bear to see the calamity that is coming on my people? Or how can I bear to see the destruction of my kindred?' (8:6).

The story goes on to recount how the tables were turned, with the Jews killing their enemies on the day originally

appointed for their own slaughter, resulting in the insti-
tution of the feast of Purim. Perhaps as a consequence
of her secular position, Esther assumes authority in this,
sending out letters commanding the observance of the feast
and detailing the ways in which it is to be kept. Like Deborah, therefore, she takes on both a role of leadership
and a role of recording events – or at least their liturgical
outcome: 'The command of Queen Esther fixed these prac-
tices of Purim and it was recorded in writing' (9:32). Her
royal position and her decision to speak out also result in
the elevation of Mordecai to be a wise leader of his people
(and presumably one acceptable to God), who 'sought the
good of his people and interceded for the welfare of all his
descendants' (10:3).

So, for all the literary embellishment of her story, Esther
can be seen using her influence and speaking out powerfully
on behalf of her people (despite her initial hesitation),
thereby significantly affecting their history, both in ensur-
ing their safety in the short term and in establishing and
recording a permanent religious festival. One feminist critic
has gone further and suggested that 'the text may stand for
values that are timeless, such as the honouring of Esther's
decision to plead for her people at the possible cost of her
life';[3] while liberation theologians have argued that the
book 'offers hope and support for the many minorities
who wish to live this way in modern pluralistic societies',
and have noted that for Esther God remains the 'well-
spring of all her positive actions'.[4] So however much her
detractors may see Esther as merely employing 'feminine
wiles' with her husband, and in a largely fictitious setting at
that, she remains a significant voice among Old Testament
women.

Speaking to Influence the Powerful: Catherine of Siena (1347–80)

St Catherine of Siena had never intended to get caught up in public activity. Born in 1347, she decided at the age of six to dedicate her life to Christ, and never wavered from her intention. At fifteen she defied her parents' wish for her to marry, and two years later was admitted to a group of Third Order Dominican lay women in Siena, to embark on a life of solitude and silence. However, her life changed course when in 1368 she felt called to leave her solitary life in order to serve others. It is probably also significant that she had learned to read, something which as the daughter of a local dyer she had had no opportunity to do previously, and which would have given her insight into the effective use of words.

Catherine duly served the sick and suffering, most notably when the Black Death hit Siena in 1374, and this, coupled with her increasingly intense mystical experiences, led her to speak out for reform in the church, through which alone, she believed, those whom she served could be saved. By the 1370s Catherine was attracting a considerable following, thanks to her ministry to the sick and dying, her reported miracles, and her life of holiness. So when she started sending letters to national and religious leaders, her reputation was such that they took notice and on occasions sought her advice.

Catherine lived in turbulent times. Two things in particular troubled her. The first was that European Christian leaders were engaged in conflicts with one another when she felt that together they ought to undertake a new Christian crusade against their common enemy in the Holy Land (something which never in fact materialized). And the second, much more crucially, was the state of the papacy. Since 1309 the popes had lived in Avignon in southern

France. Catherine was tireless in urging Pope Gregory XI
to return to Rome, which he did in 1377. But on his death
the following year the Church was torn in two as rival
popes were elected by the cardinals – Urban VI by the
Roman faction and Clement VII by the French faction.
Catherine turned her attention to supporting Urban, but
she died only two years into the 'Great Schism' which
continued until 1417.

Catherine shares with biblical women an extraordinary
forthrightness, born of her conviction of her divine calling.
Pope Gregory XI in particular suffered under her rebukes
for cowardice and selfishness as she implored him to go
back to Rome. One of her letters written in 1376, the year
in which the city of Florence rebelled against the papacy,
begins after scant greeting:

> I long to see you a courageous man, free from any
> cowardice or selfish sensual love in regard to yourself
> or any of your relatives. (222)[5]

Catherine is forceful in her calls for him to act decisively:
'Up then, father; don't sit still any longer!' (217), and her
hints at his weakness are unmistakable: 'Regarding your-
self,' she writes, 'try to go confidently' (267).

In spite of this Catherine remains conscious that she is
under papal authority, and she often softens her remarks
with protestations of humility and unworthiness. Not
so when she writes to secular leaders. To Charles V of
France, referring to his war with Louis, Duke of Anjou,
she says:

> What an abomination before God that you should
> be making war against your brother and leaving
> your enemy alone ... Enough of this stupid blindness.
> (239)

while in a letter to Louis she is critical of his luxurious lifestyle and urges him to 'make ... an effort to amend your life' (241).

However harsh her words may be, Catherine never loses sight of her conviction that they are from God. Her letters to Gregory are full of biblical imagery and at times read more like sermons. She is particularly fond of the image of sheep and the shepherd (good or bad) and appeals to the Pope to follow the example of Christ and the apostles. Even so, a hint of reproach remains:

> I long to see you a good shepherd ... for I see the infernal wolf carrying off your little sheep and there is no one to rescue them. So I am turning to you, our father and shepherd, begging you in the name of Christ crucified to learn from him who with such blazing love gave himself up to the shameful death of the most holy cross to save this little lost sheep, the human race, from the devil's hands. (200–1)

But her full wrath is reserved for the Pope's rivals back in Italy, the 'bad pastors and administrators' whom she describes as 'devils incarnate' and fearful like Pilate 'who killed Christ so as not to lose his authority' (205).

Catherine also used her way with words to give encouragement and the promise of her prayers. In her final letter to Gregory before he arrived back in Rome she says:

> Let your heart rejoice, for in the many contrary things that have happened or will yet happen the deeds of God are surely being done. (266)

And she concludes:

> Find encouragement and confidence in the true servants

of God – I mean, in their prayers, for they are praying
and interceding much for you. I humbly ask for your
blessing, and so do your other children. Keep living in
God's holy and tender love. (267)

It is not certain whether Catherine ever learned to write,
and most of her letters and her mystical writings seem to
have been dictated. Perhaps the action of dictating allowed
her passion to be expressed more forcefully than it would
have been if she had been writing the words down herself.
Certainly she used her influence to say what had to be said
and she said it clearly to those in power, with an integrity
that came from her own life of holiness. In that, she was
a worthy successor to Deborah, while taking the opportunities open to her as Miriam did, and echoing the urgency
of the message of the women who were witnesses to the
resurrection.

Lavinia Byrne and the Ordination of Women

I declare that the Church has no authority whatsoever
to confer priestly ordination on women and that this
judgment is to be definitively held by all the Church's
faithful.
                    Pope John Paul II, *Ordinatio Sacerdotalis: On
                    reserving priestly ordination to men alone* (1994)

You cannot go through life not saying what you think
. . . I have to do what I believe is God's will.
          Lavinia Byrne, BBC radio interview (January 2000)

As someone who was received into the Institute of the
Blessed Virgin Mary at the age of seventeen, it may be
that, not unlike Catherine of Siena, Sister Lavinia Byrne
found that a call to speak out has taken her where she
never intended to go. In recent years she has become a

familiar voice on national radio and a prolific writer; but it has been her conviction that God is calling women to the priesthood in the Roman Catholic Church which has attracted the most attention, not all of it welcome.

In a book on women's ordination entitled *Woman at the Altar*,[6] which was published almost simultaneously with the Pope's Apostolic Letter condemning such ordination, Lavinia Byrne traces the debate on the issue back to the Second Vatican Council of 1964, which presented a particular view of baptism as the universal call to holiness of all the baptized. She interprets this as meaning that every Christian is now 'part of the "A" team', a category formerly reserved for priests and nuns. Among other things, this seemed to demand a fresh look at women and their ministry. Thirty years on, Byrne's book argues:

> The ordination of women to the priesthood is the logical conclusion of all the recent work of Catholic theology about women and, in particular, about the holiness of the baptized. It is not an aberration from what the Church teaches but rather a fulfilment of it.[7]

The years of debate, helped along by the 1989 decision of the Church of England to ordain women to the priesthood, led only to the reaffirming of the Roman Catholic Church's argument that priestly ordination was reserved to men alone. But Byrne has continued to speak out, firm in her belief that God is calling women to the priesthood in the Roman Catholic Church, while recognizing that such a step will inevitably prove costly to the Church to which she herself remains fully committed. The call to priesthood, she writes,

> . . . expose[s] women to the very fabric of God's dealing with the world. We are invited to stand at the place

where God and the world are in conversation with each other, and where women are needed both to pronounce judgement and then to be advocates of reconciliation and wholeness. The presence of women at the altar is an extraordinarily powerful sign of what it is that is done at that place.[8]

Byrne's arguments tend to be couched in terms such as these; she is deeply reflective, theologically informed, and conscious of the profound change in the way of looking at women theologically which ordination would entail. There is no strident feminism here – rather, a thoughtful critique of what feminism has contributed to the debate as well as its shortcomings.

Nevertheless, however well put, such statements go against the party line, and early in 2000 Byrne was asked by officials of the Roman Catholic Church to make a public statement supporting *Ordinatio Sacerdotalis*. Unable to do this with integrity, she had to leave her order so as to be able to speak out freely, though not without some harsh words for her accusers: 'We have a right to have a debate and that debate has been silenced. That's not a very Catholic thing to do – it smacks of the Inquisition.'[9] She described her emotions on leaving her order variously as having felt as if she had one hand tied behind her back, and feeling as if a lead bar had been lifted. She will no doubt continue to speak out for women's ordination, though whether her voice will be as effective outside her order remains to be seen.

At the same time as speaking out herself, Lavinia Byrne has done much to enable other women's voices to be heard as well. Three books published between 1991 and 1995 – *The Hidden Tradition*, *The Hidden Journey* and *The Hidden Voice* – present women's spiritual writings through selected texts and editorial comment. Byrne's own conviction is evident in the introduction to *The Hidden Voice* (1995):

> The 'hidden voice' of women is now a public and authoritative one. It offers a new conversation with the theological, social and political concerns of our own times.[10]

It is this last volume of the trilogy which, in presenting women's voices specifically, has most to do with the question of women's ministry in the church. It includes extracts from women such as Catherine Booth (discussed in Chapter 3 below), who describes women engaged in preaching the gospel as 'among the most amiable, self-sacrificing and unobtrusive of their sex', and the Quaker preacher Frances Willard, who observed in 1888:

> It is very interesting to me to see how God is providentially making room for us, in spite of the iron-clad prejudices of the churches.[11]

So Byrne uses voices of women of the past to add weight to those in the present, and develops the theme, which can already be discerned in the letters of Catherine of Siena, that women's ministry brings healing to the church. But this also provokes reaction:

> Theology may be built out of experience. With the admission of women to the preaching ministry of the Church, the base of this experience was broadened. But so too was the base of reaction to it.[12]

This has not been without personal cost. On the publication of her most recent book, *The Journey is my Home*,[13] she mentioned her hurt at being 'treated as though I was a problem rather than a human being or a loyal church worker'.[14] Yet she went on to say that she remains loyal to 'the Church that I support, I subscribe to, and to which I give my full and confident and loyal obedience'.

*   *   *

Across the centuries, from biblical times to the present day, women's voices may be heard in a wide range of contexts, calling people to action (Deborah), drawing attention to life-changing events (Esther, the women at the tomb) or seeking to change individuals or institutions (Miriam, Catherine of Siena, Lavinia Byrne). Their manner of speaking is generally forthright, but typically is also deeply reflective. Yet women who are called by God to speak out are not guaranteed a warm reception. Even those who reported Jesus' resurrection at first met with scorn: according to Luke's account, their words 'seemed to [the apostles] an idle tale, and they did not believe them' (Luke 24:11). In this respect the Old Testament characters of Deborah, Miriam and Esther fared rather better – even Miriam was listened to and taken seriously. While medieval women tended to attract respect because of their social class or holy lifestyle, many who came after them met with hostility or indifference. As we shall see, this will be even more apparent in the case of women who have been called to speak out in the course of exercising other gifts, in particular gifts of prophecy and of leadership.

2

Women Taking Action

As the Old and New Testaments unfold, there are plenty of examples of women who, often contrary to the custom of their time, engage in bold actions. If this does not seem to be the impression we are generally given, it may be because the names of a significant number of these women are not recorded, and also because the fact that they have taken any action at all often has to be inferred from the context. The Gospel of Luke, for example, refers in passing to a number of women who followed Jesus in his itinerant ministry, without drawing any attention to the courage that acting in this way would have demanded of them.

Ironically, the outstanding woman of action whose story we do know in full, Judith, is the heroine of a book which not only is not part of the biblical canon, but is probably also a work of fiction. Even so, it is reasonable to assume that the characteristics she displays were admired by the book's original readers and that her actions were a source of national pride.

Judith: 'The Great Pride of the Nation' (Judith 8–16)

Like his probable contemporary the writer of the book of Daniel (which most people now agree dates from the second century BC), the author of Judith sets his story in the days of King Nebuchadnezzar, whom he calls King of the Assyrians. Historical accuracy, however, is not his main concern, since we are also told that the people have 'recently returned from exile' (Judith 4:3). The first part of the story (chapters 1 to 7) describes how Holofernes, Nebuchadnezzar's general, invades nations to the west because they refuse to join him in war against the Medes. By chapter 7 Holofernes has reached the fictitious Jewish town of Bethulia 'to seize the passes up into the hill country and make war on the Israelites' (7:1), his plan being to starve its people into submission. By the time Judith appears on the scene the people are in despair, though Uzziah, one of the town magistrates, urges them to hold out for five more days: 'by that time the Lord our God will turn his mercy to us again, for he will not forsake us utterly' (7:30).

Judith is introduced at the beginning of chapter 8 and is by implication the answer to Uzziah's call to faith. She is noted for three things: her beauty, the wealth left to her by her late husband, and her reputation for faith and wisdom: 'No one spoke ill of her, for she feared God with great devotion' (8:8). All these things will be important in the action she is shortly to undertake on her people's behalf.

Judith's reaction to Uzziah's negotiation of a further five days in the face of the people's desire to surrender is to condemn him publicly for testing God in this way, as she reminds the town's rulers of the nature of God who is 'not like a human being, to be threatened, or like a mere mortal, to be won over by pleading . . . he will hear our voice, if it pleases him' (8:16, 17). In the manner of the ancient prophets, Judith reminds the people of God's actions in the past: 'In spite of everything let us give thanks to the Lord our God, who is putting us to the test as he did our ancestors' (8:25). It is a long speech and Uzziah appreciates her wisdom, but reminds her that he is bound by an oath to the people. Instead he asks Judith as a devout woman to pray for them, but she has other plans: it is time to take action.

Before embarking on her dramatic enterprise, however, Judith does pray – and at some length – asking that God will crush the arrogance of the Assyrians 'by the hand of a woman' (9:10), in order to fulfil the greater purpose of upholding his reputation:

> Let your whole nation and every tribe know and under-
> stand that you are God, the God of all power and might,
> and that there is no other who protects the people of
> Israel but you alone! (9:14)

With her mission thus rooted in prayer, Judith leaves Bethulia, no longer dressed as a widow but 'in the festive attire that she used to wear' (10:3), showing off her beauty to the best possible advantage. Interestingly the town's rulers seem to realize what she is about, and ask that God will bless her plans. Judith and her maid set out for the Assyrian camp where Judith presents herself as a traitor, demanding to see Holofernes to tell him the best way to capture Bethulia. Judith quickly wins Holofernes' approval: 'No other woman from one end of the earth to the other looks so beautiful or speaks so wisely' (11:21).

For three days Judith remains at the enemy camp, eating her own food which she has brought with her and generally keeping apart from the Assyrians as she waits for God to guide her. The following day, though, she agrees to eat and drink with Holofernes, leading him to suppose that she will give herself to him. She gets the commander rolling drunk and, once alone with him, in a supreme act of strength cuts off his head. In a gruesome, but necessary, touch, she puts the head in the bag which had previously held her food and returns home. In the military action that follows, the Assyrians take fright at the sight of Holofernes' head displayed on the parapet of Bethulia, paving the way for a great victory for Israel.

In this fast-moving, action-packed story the heroine never loses sight of God. It is he who protects her in her daring undertaking and gives her the strength to act, and it is to God that Judith gives all the credit:

> Praise God, who has not withdrawn his mercy from the house of Israel, but has destroyed our enemies by my hand this very night! (13:14)

When it is all over, though, the people acknowledge that Judith has, under God, saved the nation (15:10) and she is honoured accordingly. Judith's response, like that of Deborah, consists of a song of thanksgiving, which comprises most of chapter 16, telling her own story and glorifying the strength and vengeance of God.

The closing verses of the Book of Judith reiterate the qualities which have enabled her to act so dramatically on behalf of her people: her beauty attracts many suitors but she never remarries (16:22); she shows concern for the welfare of others, giving her maid her freedom and distributing her considerable property before her death (16: 23, 24); and she continues to be held in high esteem years later (16:21). The most telling tribute comes in the final verse of the book: 'No one ever again spread terror among the Israelites during the lifetime of Judith, or for a long time after her death' (16:25), a reminder of her courage on her people's behalf and under the constant protection of God himself.

Women Disciples

It is indisputable that for many of the women who became followers of Jesus, their faith compelled them to action outside their immediate circle. We have to look carefully for signs of their presence among the people who literally followed Jesus and among those who had a ministry in the early church, but the number of almost passing references to women suggests that there were plenty of them.

As we shall see again, it is Luke's Gospel which shows a marked interest in the presence and role of women in Jesus' ministry. When Jesus sets out on his second preaching tour (Luke 8:1–3) the evangelist states that he takes not only the twelve with him, but also 'some women who had been cured of evil spirits and infirmities' (8:2) and he goes on to name three of them: Mary Magdalene, Joanna, the wife of Herod's steward, and Susanna. There were also, says Luke, 'many other' women present whose action took the form of financial support (8:3).

When Jesus is on his way to Calvary, Luke alone records that among the crowds following him were 'women who were beating their breasts and wailing for him' (23:27). These women may not necessarily have been disciples, although they went out of their way to be with Jesus, and they inspire the only words of Jesus recorded on his terrible journey: 'Daughters of Jerusalem, do not weep for me, but weep for yourselves and for your children' (23:28ff.).

Finally, on the day of resurrection, after Luke has recounted how 'Mary Magdalene, Joanna, Mary the mother of James and the other women with them' (24:10) had come to tell the men about the angel at the empty tomb, the two disciples on the way to Emmaus say almost casually to their unknown companion that it was 'some women of our group' who astounded us (24:22). This surely must suggest that the presence of women among the followers of Jesus was accepted and normal, and probably there was a fair number of them. Look closely at the Gospels, then, and there are plenty of women around.

The same is true of the early church. At the beginning of Acts, for example, when the disciples were praying in the upper room before Pentecost, 'certain women, including Mary the mother of Jesus' were with them (Acts 1:14). Subsequent evidence for the active ministry of women is to be found at the end of some of Paul's letters, when he sends greetings to or from his associates. The last chapter of Romans is little more than a list of such greetings. First among the people named is the deaconess Phoebe (Romans 16:1), for whom Paul asks that 'you may welcome her in the Lord as is fitting for the saints, and help her in whatever she may require from you, for she has been a benefactor of many and of myself as well' (16:2–3). It seems that it was Phoebe who was entrusted with taking Paul's letter to Rome and the reference to her helping many might also imply wealth and independence. The list of other greetings includes Prisca, who is mentioned again at the end of 1 Corinthians (16:19) and whom we shall consider further in the next chapter. Then there is Mary 'who has worked very hard among you' (Romans 16:6), and later Julia (16:15), about whom Paul says nothing.

Philippians 4 has an intriguing reference to two women who have had a disagreement: 'I urge Euodia and I urge Syntyche to be of the same mind in the Lord' (Philippians 4:2). Their quarrel seems to distress Paul as he asks others to help them resolve it, for their work is important: 'they have struggled beside me in the gospel together with Clement and the rest of my co-workers, whose names are in the book of life' (4:3).

It is tempting to conclude from all this that the presence of women active in ministry was sufficiently common for the New Testament writers not to feel they had to make particular mention of them. If Paul, the alleged though unproven misogynist, pays them such respect, their contribution to the early church must have been invaluable.

Jeanne d'Arc (c. 1412–31): The Maid of Orleans

> *Promoter:* Don't you think you would have done better to go on with your sewing and spinning beside your mother?
> *Joan:* I had something else to do, my Lord. There have always been plenty of women to do women's work.
> *Inquisitor:* ... Did it never occur to you to consecrate your life to prayer, supplicating that heaven itself should expel the English from France?
> *Joan:* God likes to see action first, my Lord. Prayer is extra.
>
> Jean Anouilh, *The Lark*, Part II[1]

It is hard to imagine one woman who is viewed so differently, depending on which side of the English Channel one happens to be. To the English fighting the Hundred Years War, she was a thorough nuisance, and, to some extent, someone to be feared, since she was instrumental in carrying out the relief of Orleans and having Charles VII crowned at Reims. A year after this, though, in 1430, she was captured by the Burgundians and sold to the English, who had blamed their military failures in France on Jeanne's so-called witchcraft.[2] After a trial full of illegalities, Jeanne was convicted as a witch, and burnt at Rouen in May 1431.

To the French, however, the Maid of Orleans is a national heroine. Some years after her death she was fully exonerated when in 1455 an ecclesiastical court reversed the English guilty verdict, and in 1920 she was canonized. Yet French memories are long. When I was an English language *assistante* in northern France in the late 1960s I was constantly being greeted by French schoolchildren with the accusation, 'You killed Jeanne d'Arc!'

Jeanne was the daughter of a peasant farmer at Domremy in the Champagne area. Probably the youngest of five children she never learned to read or write, but seems to have been a devout child. When she was thirteen she began to hear voices, whom she identified as St Michael (accompanied in her visions by some of his angels), St Margaret and St Catherine. In October 1428 Orleans was invaded by the English and Jeanne's voices became more urgent, calling her to go and free the city from its occupiers. She is said to have objected: 'I am a poor girl; I do not know how to ride and fight', only to receive the reply, 'It is God who commands it.'[3] And in January 1429 Jeanne duly set out from Domremy.

Jeanne succeeded in convincing the local commander of her calling. Dressed in a man's costume she then set out to see the dauphin, the future Charles VII, at Chinon, where she recognized him instantly even though he had assumed a disguise to test her. He too was convinced by her, not least because she spoke to him of a secret he alone knew (which is thought to have been his hidden doubts about his own birth). It was only to Charles that Jeanne described her visions, refusing even at her trial to give any indication of the saints' outward appearance.

At the head of her own troops Jeanne led the offensive which took Orleans from the English. She then moved on to Patay on the Loire, and after that Troyes, taking the towns with ease. At Reims she had Charles crowned in the cathedral on 17 July 1429. Having achieved her main objective, Jeanne moved on towards Paris, where the tide began to turn against her. She was defeated at Compiegne, and the apathetic king signed a truce with the Duke of Burgundy and left Jeanne to her fate.

Jeanne knew herself to be wholly called to action. Her visions were geared to one thing and one thing only: the victory of the French and of the dauphin. Although she was esteemed for her chastity, she did not make any claims to being a saint, and her divine mission was a concrete, earthly one. All the time she was notching up military successes, the French nobility and church leaders backed her to the hilt, even claiming to share her visions themselves. But when she failed to keep her promise to take Paris, her followers rapidly became disillusioned. Marina Warner attributes this to the restricted nature of Jeanne's prophetic vision:

> Her predecessors in the prophetic tradition had foretold all manner of wonders and horrors attendant upon the arrival of the Anti-Christ. If Joan had followed them, if she had expressed her knowledge of the supernatural in unverifiable imagery and language, if her utterances had lent themselves to wider interpretation, if she had been more otherworldly, she would have been able to command credence for longer.[4]

One of the tactics of Jeanne's accusers at her trial was to try to force her into an admission of heresy. She was questioned about her own sinfulness, whereupon she replied that she did not think she would have received her visions if she had been in a state of sin. Warner comments:

> This reply was ambiguous, for it implied that she knew herself to be in a state of grace through her visions, not through the Church and God's sacraments. So Joan did not escape the charge, made commonly in fourteenth- and fifteenth-century Inquisition trials, that like a heretic she believed herself to be in a state of grace, however much she sinned. She herself never made any assertion of that order.[5]

There were also attempts to draw her into the arguments arising out of papal schism. While she was preparing for battle outside Paris, Jeanne received a letter from the

Comte d'Armagnac, asking her which pope he should support. Jeanne replied in haste, saying she would let him know. This was a mistake, since orthodox Christianity recognized only the pope in Rome. At her trial she seemed bemused, asking if there were really two popes. Without describing her visions she insisted that they were real: 'I saw them with these very eyes, as well as I see you.' A further charge against her was her apparent disregard for the church, preferring to carry out her mission through the temporal powers. But as a country girl she knew little of such matters, and in the end her innocence, coupled with her wholehearted commitment to act in the French cause, condemned her.

At her trial Jeanne revealed a simple piety and sound good sense. Yet in the end her visions were declared 'false and diabolical'. She signed a retraction and was briefly reprieved, but those seeking her death declared that she would be convicted as a heretic if she continued to dress as a man, which she did, probably for her own protection. Once again she was sentenced and she was burnt at the stake the next day. It was not only the English who were glad to be rid of her. In the same month as her death, May 1431, sermons were preached in Paris justifying the charge of heresy against her and her execution.

Jeanne, who was geared to action, was not used to talking theology or, indeed, to public speaking. She was very far from being a mystic who contemplated supernatural mysteries. Yet her followers in their enthusiasm would invent miracles around her and often during her lifetime treated her as a saint. Perhaps if she had been older, better educated and more worldly wise, she would have acted differently. But like Judith, her patriotism was divinely inspired, and like the women disciples, when the call came, despite her young age, she had really no choice but to act.

Caroline Chisholm (1808–77): Action for Australia

> From babies who had but a week or two of life behind
> them to crooked old men and women who seemed to have
> but a week or two of life before them; and from plough-
> men bodily carrying soil out of England on their boots,
> to smiths taking away samples of its soot and smoke upon
> their skins; every age and occupation appeared to be
> crammed into the narrow compass of the 'tween decks.

Charles Dickens, *David Copperfield*
(1849–50), ch. 57

This was the scene at Gravesend as Mr and Mrs Micawber
set out for a new life in Australia. Charles Dickens' characters and their adventures are of course among the most
familiar in English literature; but what is less well known
is that he owed much of his vision of Australia and the
opportunities it offered to a remarkable woman, Caroline
Chisholm.

*　　　*　　　*

Caroline was born Caroline Jones, and enjoyed a happy
childhood in the countryside near Northampton. When
she was twenty-two she married a Scottish lieutenant,
Archibald Chisholm, then serving in the Madras Infantry
in India. This changed her life in two ways: it was the
beginning of a life of adventure and new experiences overseas, not just in India but also in Australia, and, shortly
after her wedding, she adopted her husband's Catholic
faith. This was no mere formality. Caroline's biographer,
Joanna Bogle, comments:

> She seemed to find that her new-found Catholicism
> rested comfortably on the solid Evangelical background

of her childhood, but doubtless adding to it the note of warmth and personal relationship with God that had been lacking in the stiff formality of the Anglican worship of the day.[6]

In a non-ecumenical age, Caroline's openness to other people's beliefs and ideas, whether Christian or not, was to be remarkable.

It was as an officer's wife in Madras that Caroline was first able to develop her talent for organization. She was struck by the difference between the comfortable position of officers' families and the difficult lives of the families of ordinary soldiers, particularly the children who were not given any formal education. So the privately educated Caroline established a school for soldiers' daughters, teaching them skills and generally preparing them for life.

The Chisholms' lifelong connection with Australia began when Archibald and Caroline and their two young sons spent a period of leave in Sydney in 1838. Joanna Bogle describes New South Wales at the time as a mixed society, made up of English convicts alongside farmers and traders, often the younger sons of prosperous British families, who had settled there freely. There was, she notes, already a sense that the convict era was coming to an end. But there were huge social problems, which could be attributed in particular to the fact that men outnumbered women by ten to one (47). As a result, family life among the settlers, especially in the bush, was relatively rare, and the birthrate was necessarily very low.

The human and social problem that Caroline made her own was the plight of young girls arriving in Sydney without jobs or resources. They may have come to escape life in the workhouse back home, but on arrival they found all too often that prostitution was their only means of survival. With Archibald's support for her work (support which was to remain constant throughout their married life) Caroline established a home for emigrant girls, where she settled the new arrivals until she had found them domestic employment with local Sydney families.

When Archibald's prolonged Australian leave came to an end, the couple agreed that he would return to India alone, leaving Caroline to cope by herself for the next four years with her young family and her increasingly demanding work with emigrants. Caroline knew that she had to get her work properly organized if she was going to meet the pressing needs of newly arrived immigrants. Some years later she described how she felt called to do this:

> On Easter Sunday, I was enabled . . . to make an offering of my talents to the God Who gave them. I promised to know neither country nor creed, but to try to serve all justly and impartially. I asked only to be enabled to keep these poor girls from being tempted, by their need, to mortal sin; and resolved that to accomplish this, I would in every way sacrifice my feelings – surrender all comfort – nor in fact consider my own wishes or feelings but wholly devote myself to the work I had in hand. I felt my offering was accepted and God's blessing was on my work: but it was His will to permit many serious difficulties to be thrown in my way, and to conduct me through a rugged path of deep humiliation. (58–9)[7]

Her first step was to ask the Governor for a building. At first he demurred, though he was impressed by Caroline herself:

> Mrs Chisholm is tall, stately in her bearing, ladylike in her manners. Her face beaming with kindness, her voice is musical and she speaks fluently.[8]

Eventually he gave in and let her have the Immigration
Barracks:

> She was quite forceful but in a very pleasant and femi-
> nine way. I also think she was intensely practical so
> when she came to talk to a bureaucrat or Government
> official, they were always amazed first of all how practi-
> cal she was and secondly as to what she'd already done
> before she got in their door. So that it was very hard
> for them to deny.[9]

Over the next few years Caroline's work prospered. Not
content with settling girls in Sydney, she undertook excur-
sions into the bush, where unmarried farmers needed
domestic help – arrangements which frequently resulted in
marriage. But Caroline was also conscious of the need for
change at a higher level, and she began work on a report
for authorities in London, which argued for free and well
supervised emigration, including passage for emigrants'
families:

> She was driven on by a strong sense of urgency. There
> was something so tragic about this great, sunlit, potenti-
> ally abundant land being a source of sorrow and
> deprivation instead of hope and fulfilment. (75)

In 1845 Archibald retired from the army on health
grounds and thereafter gave himself wholeheartedly to
supporting his wife's work. This was the opportunity for
the couple to return home, and they settled in London
for the next few years. Here Caroline busied herself with
petitioning government officials and publishing pamphlets.
She succeeded in winning a free passage for a number of
wives and children to be reunited with their menfolk in
Australia, and, at the height of the Irish famine, she was

concerned to contrast poverty at home with the opportunities in New South Wales.

To facilitate free emigration, Caroline and Archibald established the Family Colonization Society, which offered families interest-free loans to cover part of their cost, and which was free from the restrictions imposed by government. As this grew, Archibald returned to Australia to administer the scheme from that end and settled in Melbourne. Meanwhile Caroline was spending her time at home tracking down members of divided families and she soon became a public figure. In 1853 she was honoured by the Pope, and before she went out to join Archibald a public collection was organized for her. Until then she had received no money for her work, either at home or in Australia. As always she remained faithful to her Easter Day pledge to help people regardless of country and creed, and when she set out for Melbourne she took a group of Jewish girls with her. From Melbourne the couple moved to Sydney before eventually returning to Liverpool, where Caroline was given a Civil List pension of £100 per year. She spent the last years of her life in London, and when she died in 1877 she was buried back home in Northampton.

Caroline seems to have been the very model of an early development worker. When she and Archibald first arrived in Sydney Archibald had lent money to some penniless Scottish immigrants; but it was Caroline who suggested that they spend it on setting up a wood-cutting business in order to become self-sufficient. She was a great organizer, but she was also a family person, and it was the respect for family life which she was so concerned to uphold in the rich new colony. Her faith was crucial, although she had to fight against the rumour that she was part of a Catholic plot to take over Australia:

She was clearly a woman of great spiritual resources, and she succeeded in passing on her Catholic faith to her children in such a way that their subsequent lives were similarly moulded and formed by it. She had to face taunts because of her adherence to a Church which was often misrepresented to her fellow countrymen, but she did not waver. (155)

In the strength of her faith she was able to engage almost single-handedly in actions which influenced the future life of a whole nation. This was acknowledged by the Catholic Bishops of Australia when in 1976 they issued the following prayer:

Heavenly Father, in your boundless love you provide for your people. In the person of Caroline Chisholm you cared for the women of this growing nation and implanted here a concern for the dignity of womanhood. Let her life of selfless concern be a model and an inspiration for Christian people today. We ask this through Jesus Christ Our Lord. (151)

*　　*　　*

Women are motivated to act in the world for many different reasons. Judith acted dramatically on behalf of the people of God, while the earliest women disciples through their activities were instrumental in spreading the gospel and in establishing the early church. Nationalism inspired Jeanne d'Arc, while Caroline Chisholm's concern was primarily for social justice for women, although love of her adopted country may also have played a part. Whatever the reason behind women's resolve, their example shows that, however much history may conceal it, the excellence of women is to be found again and again in direct action.

3

Family Women

Family life is never an easy option. For those who have sought to combine it with another calling, there are untold strains and tensions to be dealt with if the family is to preserve both its relational and spiritual integrity. I had not intended to draw both my modern biblical successors from the families of well-known evangelists, but that is how it turned out, perhaps because they more than most have found both aspects of their lives subject to public interest and scrutiny, and have emerged from it with credit. On the other hand, there are families in the Old Testament which in modern terminology could almost be called dysfunctional, were it not for the unseen hand of God guiding – some would say interfering with – their lives. The women in those families also come out of it with credit, if only for faithfully playing out their role in the most unusual or demanding of circumstances.

Family Struggles: The Mother and Wives of Jacob

Rebekah (Genesis 24; 25:19–26:11; 27:5–28:9)

The editor of Genesis handles the story of the marriage of Isaac and Rebekah with unusual delicacy. It begins with Abraham in his old age determined that his son should marry a woman from his own race, an Aramean, and a servant is entrusted with the task of finding her. Abraham sees this as God's will and the servant too prays for success in his undertaking.

This prayer, as so often in both the Old and New Testaments, is answered over and above what has been requested. Not only does the woman whom Abraham's envoy asks for water respond appropriately: she is also 'very fair to look upon' (24:16) and is not just any Aramean but one of Abraham's own family, the daughter of his brother Nahor. Her good nature is as evident as her beauty: she needs no prompting to offer to fetch water for the servant's ten camels, a gesture which would have meant her carrying up many jars of water from the well, over and above her own needs.

Again the servant turns to God, this time in thanksgiving, and when he meets Rebekah's brother Laban, he tells his story of divine guidance in such a way that Laban cannot refuse his request for Rebekah's hand: 'The thing comes from the Lord ... Look, Rebekah is before you; take her and go, and let her be the wife of your master's son, as the Lord has spoken' (24:51). So Rebekah travels to meet Isaac, with her family's blessing: 'May you, our sister, become thousands of myriads; may your offspring gain possession of the gates of their foes' (24:60). That this is indeed to be Rebekah's destiny is strongly hinted at in the detail that when they meet, Isaac takes her into his late mother's tent (24:67), thus installing her as Sarah's successor as the ancestor of the children of Israel.

The idyllic note soon disappears. When we next meet Rebekah she is pregnant with twins. The struggling babies cause her immense pain, and she cries out, 'If it is to be this way, why do I live?' (25:22). To this anguished plea God gives an enigmatic response:

> Two nations are in your womb,
> and two peoples born of you shall be divided;

> the one shall be stronger than the other,
> the elder shall serve the younger. (25:23)

What is left unsaid is that Rebekah herself will deepen the division between the brothers, and in her turn will be a victim of it. As they grow up the twins drive a wedge between their parents, with Isaac preferring Esau the hunter while Rebekah favours the quieter, more settled Jacob.

After the famous occasion when the starving Esau gives Jacob his birthright in exchange for some bread and soup, there is a further interruption to the family's story. The intervening episode is an encounter between Isaac and Abimelech, which incidentally reveals Rebekah's continuing beauty, as Isaac, fearing he might be killed so that the men of Gerar can take his wife, pretends that she is his sister. This is a dangerous move, but one that safeguards Rebekah's position as Israel's ancestor. The twins reappear at the beginning of chapter 27, but not before we are told that Esau, approaching middle age, has taken two Hittite wives who 'made life bitter for Isaac and Rebekah' (26:35). This ensures that Esau's descendants, who were to be Edomites, would not be inheritors of God's promise.

The family's story comes to a climax when Isaac, fearing he is close to death, wants to give Esau, the elder brother and his favourite, his blessing. Overhearing their conversation, Rebekah now emerges as a dangerous schemer when the interests of her favourite are threatened. Despite Jacob's reservations, she dresses him in Esau's clothes and, somewhat ludicrously, gives him animal skins to make his hands and neck appear hairy. She reveals the depth of her devotion to her son when he protests that his father, once he realizes he is being deceived, will give him not a blessing but a curse. 'Let your curse be on me, my son,' replies Rebekah (27:13), solemn words indeed, and Jacob allows himself to be persuaded.

It is a cruel and shameful action on Jacob's part to deceive his blind father, and for a second time Esau is forcibly deprived of what is rightfully his. Almost inevitably, Rebekah pays the price for her part in the deception. Hearing that Esau is threatening to kill his brother, she sends Jacob away, she thinks for just a short time, so that she may not lose both her sons (for if Esau had succeeded in killing Jacob he would have been forced to flee the country). In the event, Jacob is away for twenty years, so Rebekah effectively loses her favourite boy.

However, some good does come out of it all, as Esau is moved by Isaac's command to Jacob not to marry a Canaanite woman, and his third wife is much more acceptable – a cousin on his father's side of the family – and presumably spares his parents further trouble from a daughter-in-law. When much later Jacob and Esau are reunited, the hatred between them has gone and in due course they bury their father together (35:29).

Rebekah's role in all this is problematic. Was she guilty of blatant favouritism, or was she genuinely convinced that Jacob was the more suitable of the two brothers to continue the line of God's people? The disgraceful behaviour of Rebekah and Jacob in deceiving Isaac certainly had this effect, but at considerable cost to the family itself. Gerhard von Rad refers to this as a 'monstrous act of God', which almost destroys all the people concerned, and he concludes: 'God, in pursuit of his plans which had to remain concealed from all relevant persons, broke into a family and . . . seems to pass beyond its ruins.'[1]

Rachel and Leah (Genesis 29–31; 35:16–21)

In many respects history seems to be repeating itself in the story of Rachel. There is family treachery and deception, and the tale of a despised barren wife (a reminder of Sarah and Hagar, cf. Genesis 16). At the same time, though, we see in Rachel a devoted and loving wife, who displays a certain quick-wittedness to save her family when the occasion demands it.

It has been suggested that the story of Rachel and Leah is included to explain the tradition of the twelve tribes having two ancestral mothers. But, as von Rad points out, it is a story not about tribes but about people: 'It tells of women and their struggle for husbands and for descendants.'[2]

The first meeting between Jacob and Rachel is beautifully related and is strongly reminiscent of the young Rebekah meeting Isaac. Rachel too is beautiful, and Jacob is enchanted by her, to the extent that he is prepared to accept her father's excessive demand that he should first work for him for seven years. This time 'seemed to him but a few days because of the love he had for her' (29:20). His reward is a piece of blatant deception by his future father-in-law, who insists that he first marry Leah, Rachel's elder sister, who is not blessed with Rachel's sparkling eyes. In return for a further seven years of service, Jacob is allowed to take Rachel as a second wife, in spite of the later prohibition against marrying two sisters (Leviticus 18:18).

The sisters' lot is hardly an ideal one. Leah is unloved by her husband, yet God comforts her and she gives birth to four sons. Rachel remains childless and in desperation gives Jacob her maid, who bears him two more sons whom Rachel brings up. The rivalry between the sisters intensifies and, not to be outdone, Leah also gives Jacob her maid, and two more sons are born. Finally, although she thought she would have no more children, Leah has two more sons herself. It is only then that 'God remembered Rachel, and . . . heeded her and opened her womb' (30:22). Her son is Joseph, and although Rachel still prays for one more son, the rivalry and antagonism between the two sisters appears to be at an end.

Before Rachel gives birth once more, to Benjamin, the last of Jacob's sons, and dies in the process (35:16–28), there is a further twist in the tale. The girls' father, Laban, who throughout comes across as a highly dubious character, does everything in his power to stop Jacob and his family returning to their own land, even though Jacob has given him all the service he had demanded and had allowed himself to be cheated out of his wages. Rachel and Leah are under no illusions about their father: 'Are we not regarded by him as foreigners? For he has sold us, and he has been using up the money given for us' (31:15). Eventually, though, they get some measure of revenge. As the family attempts to make a run for it, Rachel steals her father's idols. When her father confronts her she is sitting on them, and demonstrates how worthless they are, saying, 'I cannot rise before you, for the way of women is upon me' (31:35). So they remain concealed in the most 'unclean' of places imaginable.

The outcome is settled by a covenant between Jacob and Laban made before God, and with a good grace Laban allows his daughters and grandchildren to go on their way. So once again the developing history of Israel has been furthered by some dubious human actions. Von Rad describes it as 'a truly unedifying thicket of passions and human characteristics'.[3] And at the heart of it are two women going about their family lives in difficult circumstances, before their story is brought to a relatively satisfactory conclusion.

In both the stories of Jacob's mother and his wives, there are tensions between siblings and between the generations. Despite the comfortable living conditions of the women concerned, being family women was not for them an easy option.

New Testament Families

The great family sagas which are so much a feature of the early history of Israel come to an end with the eventual settling of the tribes and the establishment of the kingdom. Although the Apocrypha also has its family stories, most notably that of the Maccabees in the second century BC, there is no place for such stories in the books of the New Testament. Not that families are absent: there is of course the holy family and the parents of John the Baptist, as well as the family of Martha, Mary and Lazarus, but the women who feature there tend to stand out for other reasons. In the New Testament church, though, we do have fleeting glimpses of Christian women whose family surroundings were of the utmost importance.

Priscilla (Acts 18:1–4, 18–28; Romans 16:3–5)

Priscilla and her husband Aquila were refugees from persecution. In AD 49 the Emperor Claudius had driven the Jews out of Rome and the couple moved to Corinth. The expulsion may have been related to disturbances in the Roman Jewish community over Christianity, and it is possible that Priscilla and Aquila were by then already Christians. In Corinth they established themselves as tentmakers (some sources say leatherworkers). They appear briefly in the story of the apostle Paul: he was their close friend, bound to them by a common religion and shared profession. Almost all we can deduce of Priscilla is that she must have been a hardworking wife who had known difficult times. It is sometimes said that she must have been of more noble birth than her husband, since she is always named first. Priscilla offered hospitality to the apostle while continuing to work at her tents, which presumably she and her husband did with some success. Paul used their home as a base from which to earn his living and to preach in the synagogue, where he would 'try to convince' Jews and Greeks alike (Acts 18:4).

When Paul eventually left for Syria, Priscilla and Aquila went with him. At Ephesus husband and wife reveal themselves to be evangelists. In the course of their ministry, in which they seem to be equal partners, the couple have an important meeting with Apollos, an Alexandrian Jew, who was to all intents and purposes a disciple of John the Baptist. Priscilla and Aquila accost Apollos as he speaks in the synagogue and tell him about Jesus, so 'explain[ing] the Way of God more accurately' (18:26). The couple's important work bears fruit in Achaia, where Apollos 'greatly helped those who through grace had become believers, for he powerfully refuted the Jews in public, showing by the scriptures that the Messiah is Jesus' (18:27–28).

After the death of Claudius this remarkable couple seem to have found it safe to return to Rome. They feature again at the end of the Epistle to the Romans where Paul pays them a warm tribute:

> Greet Prisca and Aquila, who work with me in Christ Jesus, and who risked their necks for my life, to whom not only I give thanks but also all the churches of the Gentiles. Greet also the church in their house. (Romans 16:3–5)

Priscilla, then, was, with her husband, an evangelist and a much travelled leader in the early church, known for her courage and notable for her hospitality. Nothing else is heard of them, but from the little we have, it is evident that without this family and their ever open home the early church would have been much the poorer.

Eunice and Lois (2 Timothy 1:5; 3:15)

Eunice and her mother Lois, of whom we hear nothing outside their family context, also had an important part to play among the leaders of the early church. It was their upbringing of Eunice's son Timothy, who is described in Acts 16:1 as the 'son of a Jewish woman who was a believer' and a Gentile father, which so formed him in the Christian faith that he went on to be Paul's right-hand man. Paul himself commends this family background, when he writes to Timothy: 'from childhood you have known the sacred writings that are able to instruct you for salvation through faith in Christ Jesus' (2 Timothy 3:15).

Earlier in his letter, Paul has commended the 'sincere faith' of Timothy's mother and grandmother which they had passed on to the boy. This formative background has been seen ever since as an early model of a Christian upbringing, which in Timothy had the most significant of long-term effects.

So in the New Testament we see women emerging who are immensely influential Christians, whether they practise their faith simply within the family or take it out to others as a family unit. They, more than the women of Old Testament families with their eventful histories, become the model for later women. However, because we have only a partial picture of them, it is still perhaps in the Old Testament that we see the everyday tensions of family living more accurately reflected, albeit in an extreme form.

Catherine Booth (1829–90) and Her Thousands of Daughters

In all nineteenth-century England there could not have been a couple in which both husband and wife held such strong opinions – and felt such an obligation to impose

them on other people ... [M]iraculously, on the rare
occasions when their views did not coincide, one of them
capitulated, so Catherine succeeded in being both a loyal
Victorian wife and mother, attendant to her husband's
wants and needs, yet at the same time an independent
spirit who corrected him when she thought him to be
wrong.[4]

Writing in *The Tablet*[5] Roy Hattersley, the most recent
biographer of William and Catherine Booth, founders of
the Salvation Army, describes Catherine as 'the stronger,
cleverer and certainly the more attractive partner in the
near-perfect Booth marriage'. Herself a preacher of considerable merit, Catherine was the mother of eight children,
and it is a testimony to her strength and theirs that all survived in a time notable for its high rate of infant mortality.

Catherine Mumford was born in Derbyshire to strict
parents. Her mother was a devout Methodist, who would
not allow her daughter to go to school until she was twelve,
because she feared that she would be exposed to wicked
influences. Reading novels and learning French were also
forbidden. This did not prevent Catherine, who shared her
mother's religious enthusiasm, from developing a formidable intellect while continuing to love and respect her
mother. She was also plagued by ill health which was to
dog her for the rest of her life, although she never let it
stand in her way.

When she met William Booth in 1852, he was to claim
that it was love at first sight, despite the considerable intellectual gap between them and Catherine's unprepossessing
physical appearance. Neither of them was a great romantic,
but as Hattersley notes, 'their commitment to each other
was instant and absolute' (46). At the time, William was
just starting out as a full-time preacher in the Wesleyan
Reform Church. Catherine had long been critical of the

Church of England's failure to inspire and retain its members, and it was not long before the newly engaged couple left the Wesleyan church for a similar reason, namely the failure on the part of some of its ministers to nurture the converts that preachers such as William were recruiting for them. Instead they joined a Congregationalist church, but when William was rejected for ordination he left that too, although Catherine remained, despite having some doctrinal difficulties with her new denomination. William's career was rescued by an offer from a Wesleyan Reform church in Lincolnshire, which led to an eighteen-month separation from Catherine – the first of many. Even so, it was not long before he changed allegiance again, this time joining the Methodist breakaway group, the New Connexion.

Meanwhile, Catherine was developing strong views on the role of women in the church, arguing that to oppose the ministry of women was to oppose the will of God. After her marriage, as William began to make a name for himself as a popular evangelist, Catherine continued to develop her views on women. At around the same time, when the couple were working and living in Yorkshire, she came face to face with the abject poverty of the working classes. These two things were to shape her future life.

In 1859 Catherine published a pamphlet written in defence of a local woman evangelist, rooting her arguments in biblical scholarship. It was not long before Catherine too, by then the mother of four, began to preach herself, inspired by the 'inward urging of the Holy Ghost' (112).

Despite his successes in evangelistic campaigns, William once again became restless in his church, while Catherine was angered by the Connexion's emphasis on overseas mission while the poor at home were destitute. The couple began an itinerant ministry, travelling across the country wherever they were invited. Once back in London

Catherine undertook a preaching ministry and missions of her own. Moved by the dockland slums she did not flinch from addressing herself directly to the prostitutes she met there. The *Wesleyan Times* reported:

> She identified herself with [the prostitutes] as a fellow sinner, showing that if they supposed her to be better than themselves it was a mistake, since all had sinned against God. (148)

When William began work at the East London Christian Mission the family had the luxury of a permanent home for the first time. The elder children were already paying the price for the constant moving around the country and lacked a good educational foundation. Catherine seems to have shared her mother's prejudices against formal education, and employed a succession of tutors. The children were often sick – possibly inheriting their mother's predisposition to illness, or maybe just as a result of constant exposure to the slums. One governess painted a rather grim picture of the Booths' family life: 'constant prayer, absolute discipline and rice pudding every day ... Competitive games were forbidden and cricket and football denounced as frivolities which distracted grown men from serious pursuits' (172). Nonetheless, the love of both parents for their growing brood should not be doubted.

East London was the start of the Booths' fast growing ministry to the poor, most of whom would not have been welcome in respectable churches and chapels, and it was there that they introduced soup kitchens. Satisfying physical hunger was seen as a necessary preliminary to satisfying people's spiritual needs (a view not shared by all modern evangelists); and it was out of the work in East London that the Salvation Army evolved. A church historian has summed up the Booths' enterprise in these words:

Booth ran his campaign on military lines. In 1878 he adopted the title of 'general' and put his followers into uniform. He expected to have complete control over his Salvation Army and to be given unquestioning obedience by his soldiers. On such terms he led them into battle against sin and vice, facing obloquy and violence. Many of them, both men and women, were assaulted and hustled every time they went out. But their courage was remarkable.[6]

It was at Catherine's insistence that prospective officers of the Salvation Army underwent proper training, and she was instrumental in having a training home set up. She was also robust in defending the Salvation Army publicly and through its new magazine *The War Cry*, and she was particularly concerned to stave off attacks on the practice of using women evangelists.

In 1882 the Booths' eldest son Bramwell married Florence Soper, a fellow Salvationist, and the occasion was used to promote the idea that he would become his father's successor. Hattersley comments:

> Bramwell's wedding provided a perfect example of William Booth's view of his relationship with the Army which he had created. He was its father and it was his family, and he genuinely believed that his blood relatives (and their husbands and wives when they acquired them) ought to be accepted as specially blessed members. (282)

Catherine presumably shared this view, since she welcomed Florence with the words 'I cannot say that I am gaining a daughter today, for this dear one is already my own spiritual child' (282).

In the 1870s Catherine had forged a friendship with the social reformer Josephine Butler, who was as concerned for the rights of women in society as Catherine was for them in the church. Together they had campaigned against the 1874 Contagious Diseases Act, which they interpreted as blaming women for prostitution, arguing that this problem was as much a social one as a moral one. A few years later the Salvation Army, led by Bramwell Booth, began a campaign to have the age of consent for girls raised from thirteen to fifteen. Catherine wrote letters to Queen Victoria and Prime Minister Gladstone on the subject, and spoke at a number of public meetings. A petition to the House of Commons asking for the age of consent to be raised still further to eighteen attracted 393,000 signatures, and was presented in the form of a piece of paper two and a half miles long. In the event the age of consent was raised to sixteen.

The 1880s were marred by two things: William was accused of misappropriating Salvation Army funds (he had no great interest or competence in financial matters), and Catherine was diagnosed with cancer. Catherine's first reaction to the news was distress that she would not be alive to nurse her husband on his deathbed. She refused surgery, apparently hoping for some other cure, whether natural or divine, and as she became increasingly sick she continued to play a leading role in running the Army. Her suffering continued for the best part of three years. Before she died Catherine prayed 'Lord, let the end be easy for Emma's [her daughter's] sake' (330). Her dying thoughts, though, were always of her wider family, the Army, and this was echoed by William, who wrote after her death, 'she will live on and on and on in the hearts and lives of thousands of her daughters' (339).

By today's standards, Catherine could not be called a devoted family woman, though she did her best to accommodate the demands of family life with the mission to which she and her husband were called. Yet it has always to be remembered that this was the golden age of emotional reticence, and probably she never publicly expressed the depths of her family feeling, or indeed her hurt at attacks on her as a wife and mother. All we can say is that her children followed faithfully in her footsteps and her huge adopted family that was the Salvation Army greatly mourned her passing. Without her William was never the same again.

Ruth Bell Graham: A 'Lost' Life?

If I marry Bill I must marry him with my eyes open. He will be increasingly burdened for lost souls and increasingly active in the Lord's work. After the joy and satisfaction of knowing that I am his by rights – and his forever, I will slip into the background . . . In short, be a lost life. Lost in Bill's.[7]

So wrote the future wife of another famous evangelist, Billy Graham, a woman who throughout her married life has devoted herself to her husband and her family, yet whose gifts have also ensured that she has won respect and acclaim in her own right.

Ruth Bell grew up in China, the daughter of a medical missionary. She attended school in what is now North Korea, but was evacuated to the United States in 1937, when she was seventeen, when war broke out with Japan. She was a child described by another missionary as being 'above average in spirituality' (21) and her ambition was to be a missionary in Tibet. From an early age she displayed a talent for writing poetry, and this is something she has continued to do throughout her life, publishing her own collection of poems, *Sitting by my Laughing Fire* (1982).

While Ruth and her future husband both came from Christian families, in some ways they could hardly have been more different. As Ruth confided to her biographer,

Patricia Cornwell, 'Billy was brought up in a house where the women did not question men, while in the Bell house, that's all we did' (79). Cornwell comments that in Billy's rural world, a woman's life revolved around her husband; while Ruth 'was accustomed to strong-willed outspoken women like her mother, Billy's authoritativeness was galling and became the couple's most volatile point' (79). If that is so, then it is not hard to imagine the inner strength which Ruth needed in order to take her place alongside her famous husband. In 1947 she expressed her feelings in a three-stanza poem which ends like this:

> So –
> love
> without clinging;
> cry –
> if you must
> but privately cry;
> the heart will adjust
> to being the heart,
> not the forefront of life;
> a part of himself,
> not the object –
> his wife.[8]

The couple's family life has been marked above all by separation. Although Ruth occasionally joined Billy on his evangelistic crusades, mostly, when their children were growing up, they were apart for long periods of time. In his autobiography Billy is particularly conscious of this and the effect his absences may have had on his children:

> This is a difficult subject for me to write about, but over the years, the BGEA and the Team became my second family without my realizing it. Ruth says those of us

who were off travelling missed the best part of our lives
– enjoying the children as they grew. She is probably
right. I was too busy preaching all over the world.

Only Ruth and the children can tell what those
extended times of separation meant to them. For myself,
as I look back, I now know that I came through those
years much the poorer both psychologically and emo-
tionally. I missed so much by not being home to see the
children grow and develop. The children must carry
scars of those separations too.[9]

Ruth's awareness of the importance of her husband's calling enabled her not only to cope with the long absences
but also to make the most of their unusual situation. Billy
Graham's biographer William Martin records a comment
by Ruth when she was asked how she and other wives
could bear their husbands being away for so long:

We know how important their work is. Then, too, we
are spared the monotony of ordinary married life ...
Every conversation is important. It's more than news
about the office or what happened at the grocery store
... It's like another honeymoon.[10]

Ruth and Billy have not hidden their concerns for their
children in these unusual circumstances. Nor does Ruth
try to pretend that her role has not involved sacrifice. Yet,
she comments:

When God asks someone to do something for Him
entailing sacrifice, He makes up for it in surprising
ways. Though He had led Bill all over the world to
preach the gospel, He had not forgotten the little family
in the mountains of North Carolina. I have watched
with gratitude as God has guided each child.(159)

Over the years Ruth has evolved her own way of being a 'family woman'. With her growing children, she was much less of a disciplinarian than her husband, and once her parents moved back to the United States it seems fair to assume that her children also experienced something of the lively questioning that had characterized her own childhood. She has also, though, allowed her own spirituality to shine through to them. Daily prayers and Bible study were an important part of family life, although Ruth was not averse to telling her husband that these times of Bible reading had to be both brief and interesting.

Ruth has also been her own woman in areas which touch on her husband's ministry. In the course of the 1954 London mission, when she joined her husband for part of the time, Ruth was criticized for wearing make-up. In her journal she prays that Billy will realize that a traditional 'Christian' appearance is in fact a stumbling block to the unconverted. 'How difficult it is for a girl to see anything attractive in Christianity when Christians look so unattractive,' she writes, adding, perceptively, 'I think it is especially easy for [people] to mistake their prejudices for convictions' (124). Billy has also valued her input to his preaching. While leading the crusade to Scotland in 1955 he wrote to Ruth:

> You have no idea how lonesome it is without you! In thinking about my message tonight, I'd give anything if you were here to talk it over with. You are the only one that ever understands my dilemma in the choice of messages. Your advice is the only one that I really trust. You have no idea how often I have listened to your advice and it has been as if it were spoken from the Lord. During the past year I have learned to lean on you a great deal more than you realize. I'll be counting the days till you arrive.[11]

There are many stories on record about Ruth's sense of humour, love of fun and practical jokes, as well as her skills in listening to strangers and her care for people in need. A telling testimony to her concern comes from a man convicted of second degree murder, who had once been in Ruth's Sunday School class: 'There is little love in prison, and Ruth had been an angel of mercy, lighting the darker places where no light, hope or love had been.'[12] Yet, says Martin, 'However extensive or effective her work with felons and orphans, Ruth's primary ministry, by all accounts, was with her children.'[13]

Ruth shared her husband's anxiety about the effect of his absence on their children, particularly on their two sons. Something of what she must have felt is expressed in her 1947 poem, 'Sons', which was written about sons of Christian workers whose fathers had to be away for extended periods of time:

> But
> what of the ones
> forsaken,
> Lord,
> even for You?
> these sons
> now grown
> who've never known
> fathers who
> had undertaken
> to leave all
> and follow You?
> Some sons,
> wounded beyond repair,
> bitter, confused, lost,
> these are the ones
> for whom

mothers weep,
bringing to You
in prayer
nights they cannot sleep –
these, Lord,
are what it cost.[14]

Both boys went through difficult times before following their parents into Christian ministry. Billy has written:

Ruth and I found out that for us, worrying and praying were not mutually exclusive. We trusted the Lord to bring the children through somehow in His own way in due time. On a day-to-day basis, however, we muddled through. But God was faithful. Today each one of them is filled with faith and fervor for the Lord's service.[15]

Ruth has always shunned media attention, and perhaps in that respect alone could hers be said to be a 'lost' life – lost to the glare of publicity and unwelcome attention of outsiders. Her many gifts are evident to anyone who troubles to seek them out. And her accomplishment as a family woman is summed up in Billy's tribute:

The secret of Ruth's survival was in her commitment – not only her marriage commitment before God of her love for me, but also her ministry commitment of the two of us to the Lord's purpose for our lives together. And Ruth will be the first to say that she loved her part – staying home with the children.[16]

4

Vulnerable Women

Dinah (Genesis 34)

> O Lord God of my ancestor Simeon, to whom you gave a sword to take revenge on those strangers who had torn off a virgin's clothing to defile her . . . so you gave up their rulers to be killed.
>
> (Judith 9:2, 3)

Dinah, daughter of the patriarch Jacob, was a woman alone in a foreign country. She is the only daughter mentioned in the Jacob stories and is commemorated in Judith's prayer in the Apocrypha. Genesis 34 recounts how Dinah, presumably hoping for some female company, set out one day to get to know the Canaanite women who were native to her family's adopted land. She never reached them. On the way she was abducted and raped by the prince's son. What follows is the story of her brothers' revenge on the local people for this violation, and nothing further is said about the fate of Dinah herself.

In the context of Old Testament history, the story of Dinah seems to have been told for a specific purpose. At one level, despite the goodwill of Shechem's people, it stresses the divide between the nomadic people of God and the settled, prosperous Canaanites – a divide which Dinah crossed at great personal cost. Seen in a historical perspective, though, the story offers an explanation for Jacob's curse on two of his sons, Simeon and Levi, and the consequent geographic separation of their descendants from the rest of the family, which is recorded in Genesis 49:

> Cursed be their anger, for it is fierce;
> and their wrath, for it is cruel!
> I will divide them in Jacob
> and scatter them in Israel.
>
> (Genesis 49:7)

In Genesis 34 Simeon and Levi become murderers: they slaughter the men of Shechem while the other brothers plunder the city, in the name of avenging their sister Dinah.

The vulnerability of Dinah takes many forms. Young and unprotected, she is obviously vulnerable to attack. Yet she is also, in a sense, the victim of her own family. Her father Jacob, who should have at least defended her interests, is a passive figure throughout: he does not seek to avenge his daughter, nor does he respond to Shechem's offer to marry Dinah, an option which might well have been attractive to her. All he does is rebuke Simeon and Levi for the trouble they cause (34:30). Dinah is, too, the victim of her own religious background. Gerhard von Rad notes that the word used for the attack on Dinah is 'an ancient expression for the most serious kind of sexual evil ... surrounding this word was the horror of a sacrilege which incriminated the whole cultic community before God'.[1] Shechem's act, despite his subsequent love for Dinah, is seen as an offence against God. And his offer of land and of other marriages with his people might also be seen as violating Israel's special relationship with God, which kept them separate from other peoples and nations.

So Dinah is a victim of much greater forces than herself, and little more than a pawn in the history of the patriarchs, unable to stand up to the force of her own family and the religion in which they have a defining role.

Bathsheba (2 Samuel 11)

Dinah first found herself vulnerable on the open road. Bathsheba was equally vulnerable. Frighteningly, though, she became vulnerable to abuse in the very place where she might have expected to feel safe – her own home. Just as Dinah's brothers were busy on the land and could offer her no protection, so Bathsheba is without her husband Uriah, who is away at war. Whether or not she had her own maids, we are not told: the point is that she is in a place where she should have been safe.

Unlike Dinah, Bathsheba does not fall victim to physical violence. Instead she is the object of what Cardinal Carlo-Maria Martini calls 'an inquisitive glance'.[2] She ought to have been safe – King David should have been away at battle too – but Cardinal Martini surmises that because of his age and a general feeling of security, David 'doesn't take the risks he used to'. If that is true, then David's security contrasts vividly with Bathsheba's lack of security, his regal power is set against her lack of power, just as Shechem's status may be contrasted with the helplessness of Dinah, the lonely foreigner.

But Uriah's absence at war and the presence of a neighbour with a roving eye are not the only reasons why Bathsheba is vulnerable. The heat and dust of the Near East meant that for health reasons people had to wash themselves a number of times in the course of the day, and the law upheld the importance of cleanliness. Furthermore, it has been argued that at the time polygamy was still possible: David might have been able to persuade himself that he was doing nothing wrong, even though it was certainly forbidden, as Walther Eichrodt puts it, 'to encroach upon his neighbour's marriage'.[3] Perhaps, then, Bathsheba did not have the unequivocal protection under the law that she was entitled to expect: she may have been compelled by law to bathe, and if polygamy was what King David had in mind, then there was little in law to prevent it. And in the end, the King's will had to win the day.

Bathsheba's vulnerability does not end once her adulterous relationship with David is established. When David has Uriah killed, 'she made lamentation for him' (2 Samuel 11:26). And in her grief she is most likely also to be the object of people's curiosity or condemnation. The message that Joab sent back to David from battle suggests that people were well aware of the real reason behind Uriah's death. Joab reminds David of what led to the death of Abimelech (recorded in Judges 9:52–54): 'Did not a woman throw an upper millstone on him from the wall?' (2 Samuel 11:21), whereupon Abimelech had his armour-bearer kill him with his sword, so that he should not be said to have died at the hands of a woman. The implication is obvious: Uriah had to die because of a woman, even if she was not his killer. Bathsheba, in the face of that widespread knowledge about her husband's death, is in a very difficult situation indeed.

Western art and literature have portrayed Bathsheba in a variety of ways. The authors of *The Bible and Literature* note how she is depicted variously as 'flawed and tragic' (in Rembrandt's portrait), a 'feisty, clever harridan' (in Joseph Heller's novel *God Knows* (1984)) and a 'chaste wife'. This last view comes from the Renaissance poet George Peele, in his 1599 poem 'The Love of King David and Fair Bathsabe', where Bathsheba says:

> Let not my beauty's fire
> Inflame unstaid desire,
> Nor pierce any bright eye,
> That wandereth lightly.[4]

Whichever view we prefer, Bathsheba's part in the story of King David poses problems for Christian theologians. If David is the forerunner of Christ, what is to be done about the Bathsheba episode? In 2 Samuel 12, following Nathan's rebuke, stress is placed on David's repentance and God's punishment in the form of the death of the couple's first son – an event which grieves them both.

Yet the Old Testament does not conceal David's great love for Bathsheba and its auspicious outcome in the birth of Solomon, whom, we are told, 'the Lord loved' (2 Samuel 12:24). This ensures Bathsheba's place in the genealogy of Joseph, husband of Mary, at the beginning of Matthew's Gospel (1:6). So for this vulnerable woman, there is much more at stake than the question of survival, as was the case with Dinah, and a place in the history of an early tribal society. For Bathsheba there is a place in the history that culminates in the birth of Christ.

The Woman of Samaria (John 4)

Like Dinah, the unnamed woman of Samaria who appears in John 4 is vulnerable on two counts. In the past she has been vulnerable as a woman – having had five husbands before her current non-marital relationship. And now she is also vulnerable as a Samaritan, that is, because of her religious and ethnic background. So in engaging in conversation with a Jewish man, she lays herself open to condemnation on both social and religious grounds. Like Bathsheba, though, this woman is given a special place in history, not as the mother of an earthly king but through her encounter with the Lord himself and her evangelistic ministry that followed.

This meeting came about because Jesus chose to take the shorter route from Judea to Galilee through Samaria, in spite of the centuries-long hostility between Jews and

Samaritans. The Samaritans were people of mixed Jewish and Assyrian blood – the result of intermarriage with Assyrian invaders. Although not recognized as Jewish by the people of Israel, the Samaritans claimed, like them, to be the true descendants of Jacob. And, incidentally, when Jesus comes into Samaritan territory, he is entering an area rich in associations with Jacob (John 4:5,6). It is this 'third race', seen by the Gentiles to be Jewish but rejected as such by the Jews, whom the woman at the well speaks for, just as Nicodemus in John 3 has already spoken as a representative of the Jews. And it is remarkable that such is the authority of Jesus that no one (including his disciples, who are surprised that he is talking to a woman) challenges him for holding a conversation with a Samaritan woman whom Jewish law considered unclean. It is Jesus who strikes up the conversation, and this breaking of the rules is not lost on the woman herself: 'How is it that you, a Jew, ask a drink of me, a woman of Samaria?' (4:9).

In the exchange that follows, Jesus allows the woman to bring up the religious differences between Jews and Samaritans, in particular the question of Mount Gerizim, regarded as sacred by her people and their assembly point on major festivals. He shows her that the worship of her people and of the Jews is inadequate, even though 'salvation is from the Jews . . . true worshippers will worship the Father in spirit and truth' (4:22, 23). And it is the woman then who, long before the disciples, begins to ask questions – 'He cannot be the Messiah, can he?' (4:29) – and spreads her news of what has happened so effectively that she becomes the first woman recorded in Scripture to bring people to Jesus. The people who approach him as a result make a confession of faith that is nothing short of amazing at this stage in the Gospel story: 'We know that this is truly the Saviour of the world' (4:42).

So a woman who represents a rejected race, and who is

even more of an outsider because of her sex and because of her marital adventures, leads people to Christ. Yet in addition, like Dinah, whose story had political reper-cussions, and like Bathsheba, who gave birth to Solomon, the woman of Samaria may be seen as having a function and an importance that goes beyond her own personal situation. She may be seen as representing not only her people (significant enough for a woman) but also their religion – an extraordinary departure for the culture of the time. There is no doubt that her conversation with Jesus has religion as its starting point. John Marsh suggests,[5] in addition, that if she stands for the Samaritan religion, her husbands represent the five nations who were brought in to repopulate Samaria after the Assyrian conquest (2 Kings 17:24), who worshipped foreign gods (17:31). Her current partner is not her husband – that is, not the true God – either.

The whole episode is overlaid with ambiguity. When the woman recognizes Jesus to be a prophet, she also draws on several meanings: is it that Jesus simply showed inex-plicable knowledge of her domestic affairs – leading her to anticipate a tirade against adultery in the style of ancient prophets? Or does she recognize in him the prophet Messiah promised in Deuteronomy 18:15? Are we on the literal plane of human marriage or a figurative spiritual plane?

Whichever interpretation is to be preferred, it is inescap-ably true that in John 4 we are presented with a woman who is vulnerable in social terms, yet who, because of her response to Jesus, is used by God for purposes that go beyond her own situation and probably her own under-standing. Although this anonymous woman is more a victim of her own and her nation's history than of her immediate surroundings (unlike Dinah and Bathsheba), her theological significance in John's Gospel as well as her more individual importance in showing Jesus' care for the women he encountered, is great indeed.

Margery Kempe (c. 1373 – c. 1440) and Her Gift of Tears

> Remember, Lord, the woman who was taken in adultery and brought before you, and as you drove away all her enemies from her as she stood alone by you, so truly you may drive away all my enemies from me, both bodily and spiritual, so that I may stand alone by you, and make my soul dead to all the joys of this world, and alive and greedy for high contemplation in God.[6]

Recording her reflections late in life, the fifteenth-century visionary, Margery Kempe of King's Lynn in Norfolk, aligns herself with the woman taken in adultery (John 8: 3–11) (see further Chapter 9 below). It is a good parallel. The woman in John's Gospel stands alone, having been discovered in the act of adultery and in full expectation of condemnation and death by stoning. Then she finds herself the subject of a public argument between religious leaders and Jesus, who declares, 'Let anyone among you who is without sin be the first to throw a stone at her' (John 8:7). As the accusers melt away the woman is left alone with Jesus and hears his words which save her both physically and spiritually: 'Neither do I condemn you. Go on your way, and from now on do not sin again' (John 8:11).

It is not surprising that Margery should have felt a particular affinity with this woman. Like her, Margery was the object of public scorn, though not just on one occasion but for most of her life, and this put her in frightening situations. By her own admission she was attractive to the opposite sex and subject to sexual temptation. Furthermore, Margery's unusual gift would often arouse suspicion and fear in other people, and isolated her from those who might have been well placed to help her. And like the woman caught in adultery, being alone with Christ was her greatest comfort and her salvation.

Margery's life story is both a racy autobiography and an account of her spiritual journey. It is told in her *Book* (1436) which she dictated, being unable to read or write herself; and her frankness about her personal life and relationships, and a similarly forthright approach to God, make it very different from the writings of other mystics, both women and men, of the medieval period.

From the outset Margery presents herself as someone marked by physical and spiritual suffering. Her opening chapters describe her physical sickness before childbirth, and her physical and mental suffering after it, when she says she 'went out of her mind and was amazingly disturbed and tormented with spirits' (41). When she was restored to health, with the help of a vision of Christ and the faithful ministrations of her husband, she reverted to worldly pursuits, until one night she heard the sound of rejoicing in heaven which caused her to weep (45). After this the rest of her life was to be marked by increasingly frequent and obtrusive weeping for all kinds of reasons: her own sinfulness and the sin of others, imagining the suffering of Christ, or simply 'out of desire for the bliss of heaven' (54). This often led to accusations of hypocrisy, as people imagined that she wept only when she was in company, and 'for advantage and profit' (48).

Margery's disturbing and disruptive behaviour aroused the hostility of clergy and laity alike. She was frequently accused of being a Lollard – the name given to the disciples of John Wyclif (who died in 1384) which originally meant 'mutterer', although according to Janet Wilson the term could also be used loosely to mean any kind of

nonconformist.[7] Wilson points out that Margery aroused
hostility both because her behaviour was considered inappropriate for a married woman and because it was hard
to understand: '[her] emotional excesses resisted any easy
classification'. So, convinced, of her calling to strive after
spiritual perfection, and in consequence to act as a spiritual
adviser to those who came to her for help, Margery was
acutely vulnerable to hostility from all sectors of society:
her own middle class, the established clergy and religious
communities, and all those whose paths she chanced to
cross. Nowhere is this more clearly exemplified than in her
account of her pilgrimages to the Holy Land, which she
undertook following the example of St Bridget of Sweden
(who died in 1373), on whose life she closely modelled her
own (see further Chapter 6 below).

It has to be said that Margery was not the kind of
travelling companion that most people would wish for.
The group she set out with soon lost patience with her,
mainly because of her behaviour at mealtimes. Margery
not only refused to eat meat, but 'she wept so much and
spoke all the time about the love and goodness of our
Lord, as much at table as in other places' (97). Alone
except for her maid, and far from home, Margery was
understandably hurt, but the others, including those she
'trusted best', refused to let her travel on with them. They
took her maid away from her, and when she begged them
to let her travel with them (for alone she could go
nowhere), they let her do so but treated her abominably:

> They cut her gown so short that it came only a little
> below her knee, and made her put on some white canvas
> in a kind of sacking apron, so that she would be taken
> for a fool. (98)

Yet in spite of this, people recognized Margery's special

character and treated her with respect, much to the annoyance of her fellow pilgrims.

At Constance, Margery was well received by the papal legate and after that she was accompanied by an old man who agreed to be her guide. Both were fearful in a strange land, not knowing the language or each other, and on this occasion Margery also recalled the story of the woman taken in adultery. So she prayed:

> Lord, as you drove away her enemies, so drive away my enemies, and preserve my chastity that I vowed to you and let me never be defiled . . . And our Lord visited her with great grace of spiritual comfort as she went on her way. (101)

At Bologna, Margery's former companions caught up with her and offered to take her back, on condition she behaved more sociably at meals, which she agreed to do. All was well for some weeks, until Margery forgot her promise not to speak of the gospel at table and was ostracized once more.

Eventually they arrived at Jerusalem, and the vivid reminder of Christ's suffering led to a new torment for Margery, not just weeping but 'crying', by which she seems to mean screaming and roaring, a condition that stayed with her for many years. Yet, she records, although these 'cryings' came upon her without warning, 'they never came without surpassing great sweetness of devotion and high contemplation' (105). At times, conscious of the spectacle she was creating, she would try and restrain herself, but to no avail:

> . . . she turned the colour of lead, and all the time it would be seething more and more in her mind until such time as it burst out. And when the body might no longer endure the spiritual effort, but was overcome with the

unspeakable love that worked so fervently in her soul, then she fell down and cried astonishingly loud. (105)

Unsurprisingly, Calvary and other sites associated with the life of Christ caused her particular suffering. She continued to be rejected by people from her own country, but other lay people and religious received her kindly and many recognized her spiritual gifts.

Margery Kempe's vulnerability resembles that of Dinah and Bathsheba as she recognizes the risks she runs as a woman on her own. She is also, like the woman of Samaria in John's Gospel, a victim of the religious and social structures of her day, to which she could hardly fail to pose a threat. Wilson comments: 'The involved interactions between the mystic and the lay and ecclesiastic communities of King's Lynn suggest that her mission became involved in a wider conflict among different beliefs, factions and ideologies.'[8] In other words, when people accepted her unusual form of piety, they were showing their dissatisfaction with the establishment. Yet, not unlike the woman of Samaria at the end of her encounter with Jesus, Margery sought only to bring people to Christ and to pray and worship through her unique spiritual gift which she believed to be from him. So she prayed:

As for my crying, my sobbing, and my weeping, Lord God Almighty, as surely as you know what scorn, what shame, what contempt, and what reproofs I have had because of them, and as surely as it is not in my power to weep loudly or quietly for devotion or sweetness, but only through the gift of the Holy Ghost, so surely, Lord, justify me so that all this world knows and trusts that it is your work and your gift, for the magnifying of your name, and for increasing of other men's love for you, Jesus. (293)

The Dawn of Hope: Genevieve de Gaulle Anthonioz

> Now I belong to those who have lost all hope. Together
> we cry out, like Christ on the cross, 'Oh, God, why hast
> thou forsaken me?'[9]

It is hard to imagine a setting in which women can be more
vulnerable than a concentration camp. Incarcerated at
Ravensbruck between 1943 and 1945 because she was
a member of 'Defense de la France', part of the French
Resistance movement, Genevieve de Gaulle spent eighteen
months in acute physical danger and in a state close to
utter despair. It was to be over forty years before she could
bring herself to write down some of her experiences.

Genevieve de Gaulle had a family name that became
increasingly famous as World War II progressed and that
may well have saved her life. Her uncle, Charles, who later
became President of France, fled the German occupation
in 1940 for London, where he set up the Free French Movement. Genevieve was one of a number of members of the
future President's family who were deported to Germany,
and this had a profound effect on him. One of his biographers wrote: 'May 1945 . . . How can one assess the shock
caused to General de Gaulle by the return of four members
of his family – above all his niece Genevieve, of whom he
was particularly fond?'[10]

By 1943, when the Resistance had emerged as a well
formed and important movement, Genevieve was twenty-
three. Her mother had died when she was only four, and
her sister had died at the age of seventeen in 1938. On
All Souls Day 1944, in the death-laden atmosphere of
Ravensbruck, Genevieve forced herself to remember her
family dead. Most recently she had lost her grandmother,
news of whose death reached her when she was in prison
in Fresnes before being sent to Germany. Yet, reflects

Genevieve, 'death isn't the worst thing here: the worst is the hate and the violence' (24). She fully anticipates dying herself and acknowledges that 'the last faces I shall see will be filled with hate and contempt' (6).

In Ravensbruck death could take many forms: random killing, the result of hideous medical experiments on the inmates, routine beating, or through illnesses brought on by the terrible conditions. At the time of her release, Genevieve was weak and emaciated, suffering from lung disease, scurvy and anaemia. Like all the women there she was vulnerable to the cold, to illness and to the hatred of her Nazi captors, who would flog women to death on a whim.

Genevieve's family name may have spared her greater suffering. As the Allies marched on Paris and the tide of war turned in their favour, it became increasingly unwise, from a German point of view, to inflict further ill treatment on a relative of Charles de Gaulle, a likely figure of power in post-war Europe. But this flicker of hope is scarcely perceptible in Genevieve's published memoir. This is how she describes her deportation:

When I was in Fresnes Prison on the outskirts of Paris, and even later during the endless voyage to Ravensbruck, once in a while there was a response to my prayers, a ray of hope. But as we entered the camp, it was as though God had remained outside. (15)

In the camp Genevieve paints a haunting picture of the women around her:

I could barely make out their unsteady silhouettes, their shaven heads, but I was thunderstruck by the vision of their faces, which has remained with me ever since. Never had I seen – on the faces of those sentenced to death, those who had been or were about to be tortured – anyone so indelibly marked by inhuman distress. These human beings, though still alive, had already lost every vestige of expression. I should have felt compassion for them, but what overwhelmed me was a feeling of utter despair. (15–16)

In her anguished state Genevieve nonetheless found a few things to comfort her: the small kindnesses which prisoners were occasionally able to do for each other; the unlikely companionship of the cockroaches in her cell; her memories of her family, of art and a world at peace. And in spite of the moments of desolation, her deep faith also sustains her:

The chant of Hail Mary comes back to me, every last word of it; Mother of mercy, our salvation, our hope, has turned her eyes toward this poor creature who is moaning and weeping. I ask her to be merciful to those who suffer or are in despair, those for whom the spectre of death looms nigh, those near and dear to me, about whom I have no news whatsoever. It's the first time since October 28 [the day of her arrival at the camp] that I have felt so close to them. (26–7)

Christmas in Ravensbruck was an opportunity for the women to try to scrape together small presents, and makeshift decorations (something which Sheila Cassidy was also to experience in a Santiago prison, see Chapter 10 below). Yet there is no respite from the suffering: 'On December 25, as on every other day, mothers will trudge to the morgue bearing the bodies of the babies for whom this is not a day of birth but of death' (31). And Genevieve develops the bleak message that for them Christmas means the very opposite of how it is generally understood:

He was born to succor the most wretched among us as He was born for the cruellest of the SS guards: for

Syllinka, for Ruth Neudeck, whom I have seen slit the
throat of an inmate with the sharp edge of her shovel.
There are no Christmas carols, even those of the angels
themselves, capable of drowning out the laments, the
screams, the cries of anger and hate. Nor is there any
way for me to get away, to transcend myself; my manger
is here in this solitary cell that separates me from the
camp but that, little by little, is filled with frightful
images and terrible rumors. (33–4)

The vulnerable state of the author is made evident by her
reaction to anything which is less horrific: 'One day I
chance upon a tiny piece of meat floating in the soup and
I burst into tears thoroughly astonished at myself for such
utter lack of self-control' (25). When she is able to leave
her cell for a short time and sees the sky again, returning
indoors is hard to bear: 'I hear the order for me to return
to my cell, to the oppressive walls of my prison, to its
darkness, its silence. When I get back inside, again I burst
into tears' (26).

In Genevieve de Gaulle it is not hard to see an echo of
the vulnerability of Dinah and Bathsheba, who were utterly
helpless at the hands of more powerful men, as well as the
sensitive faith of the woman of Samaria and later on of
Margery Kempe. And, rather as the Samaritan woman's
encounter with Jesus changed her life and made of her
an evangelist, so Genevieve de Gaulle's experience of the
'inhuman distress' of the women around her was to lead
her in new directions later in her life. She became a leader
of the ATD Fourth World International Movement, which
was founded in 1957 by Father Joseph Wresinski. 'ATD'
stands for Aid in Total Distress, and it began as a camp
for homeless families outside Paris. In the eyes of those
homeless people Genevieve recognized the same despair
that she had seen in the concentration camp, and since

then she has dedicated herself to restoring hope to the poorest people. Father Wresinski himself grew up in poverty, and the work he began in Paris has developed into an international organization working with vulnerable and disadvantaged communities worldwide, and campaigning for the rights of the poor.

Biblical women and countless women after them have been vulnerable to forces way beyond their control. Yet out of that vulnerability has often come an incredible strength from which others who are vulnerable may themselves draw strength.

5

Suffering Women

Let me not look on the death of the child. (Genesis 21:16)

Hagar (Genesis 16 and 21:8–21)

The history of God's dealings with his chosen leaders in the Old Testament not infrequently involves human casualties. This is not the result of deliberate cruelty on God's part; it tends rather to stem from shortcomings on the part of those leaders. We have already seen how David's passion for Bathsheba was also Uriah's tragedy, even though the unhappy episode eventually led to the birth of Solomon and history marched on. Much earlier, the failure of the patriarch Abraham to be fully trusting of God's promise of a son to his wife Sarah condemned the Egyptian girl Hagar to untold suffering.

There was nothing illegal in the way Sarah and Abraham treated Sarah's maid: a wife without children could legitimately provide her husband with another woman in order for them to avoid the shame of childlessness. It was, though, a breach of trust. God had promised the couple a child and they are both guilty: Sarah in proposing that Hagar take her place and Abraham in accepting her. But it is Hagar who suffers for it.

It is tempting to see Hagar's suffering as beginning when she was handed over to Abraham – when she was used by the impatient couple for their own purposes. Yet Hagar is not unhappy about this and takes pride in her pregnancy. She has succeeded where Sarah failed. Such feelings are fully in keeping with the prevailing culture which stigmatized childlessness, and Sarah might be criticized for not having anticipated the tensions that arose between them. But Hagar is still the loser. Before God intervenes, Sarah has 'dealt harshly' with the pregnant Hagar who flees far into the wilderness, until she herself receives a promise from God of many descendants and therefore of blessing.

Sarah's hostility to Hagar remains unabated once both women have given birth. This time Abraham is slightly less weak willed and does not go along with his wife's spitefulness, at least until God tells him everything will be all right. This may be because of his love for his first-born, Hagar's son Ishmael, or more likely because what Sarah proposes this time is clearly unlawful.

So yet again Hagar finds herself in the wilderness, not this time of her own free will, but driven out by the father of her child. And she ends up in the situation every parent dreads, that of having to watch her son die, or so she thinks. When God honours his promise and comes to the rescue, putting an end to her mental anguish, Hagar is not restored to the life she has left behind. From now on mother and son have to make a home in the wilderness (fulfilling God's promise in Genesis 16:12) and their separation from Abraham and Sarah is completed by Ishmael's marriage to an Egyptian.

It is hard not to see the unfortunate Hagar as a pawn in someone else's game, and that impression is reinforced by a Christian interpretation of her story, in which she becomes a purely allegorical figure. For St Paul Hagar represents the old law – she bears children 'for slavery' (Galatians 4:24), while Sarah bears Isaac, a child of promise, representing the new covenant, the gift of God's grace. 'So', exclaims Paul triumphantly, 'we are children, not of the slave but of the free woman' (Galatians 4:31).

Unlike most Old Testament, women, then, Hagar also has a role in the New Testament. She is a significant figure, too, in that she is one of only three women in the Bible who learn of the birth of a son direct from God (the other two are the mother of Samson, and Mary) as well as being one of the three women in Genesis who talk directly with God (and incidentally, unlike the other two, Eve and Sarah, she is not judged by him). But this does not conceal the fact that she suffers – as a result of her social situation, her own fear, and the spite of the woman Sarah who knows that she has done wrong in trying to secure descendants independently of the will of God.

Suffering Women and Jesus

Although cast firmly in a role that causes her to suffer, Hagar is nonetheless comforted by God's merciful intervention, first to save her and later, much to her amazement to save her son: 'Have I really seen God and remained alive after seeing him?' she exclaims (Genesis 16:13). In the Gospels Jesus reacts to suffering women in just the same way. He shows spontaneous compassion to a woman bent double for eighteen years (Luke 13:10–17) and heals her on the Sabbath; and he reacts again out of compassion to the grief of a mother whose son has died, by bringing him back to life (Luke 7:11–17). But perhaps more interesting are the women who deliberately seek relief from their suffering from Jesus, since they reveal more of themselves in the process.

The Woman with a Haemorrhage (Mark 5:24–34; Matthew 8:20–2; Luke 8:43–8)

The woman who tried to touch Jesus undetected in the hope of a cure for her debilitating illness had suffered a great deal. The very fact of bleeding continuously for twelve years would have taken an almost unimaginable toll on her body. Added to that, she was destitute: human physicians had taken all her money but had failed to heal her. She was left with nothing beyond the knowledge that her health was actually getting worse. Finally, this embarrassing, painful and exhausting condition made her a religious outcast. She was unclean not just once a month but permanently (cf. Leviticus 15:25: 'If a woman has a discharge of blood for many days, not at the time of her impurity . . . all the days of the discharge she shall continue in uncleanness'). No one could touch her or be touched by her without also becoming unclean. Hers was a truly desperate and lonely situation.

Her urge to touch Jesus' clothes is one which would have been easily recognizable to her contemporaries. In Greek and pagan culture there was a deep-rooted belief in the power of touching holy men, and that belief is seen to be continued later in some people's attitude to the apostles (see Acts 5:15; 19:11–12). At this stage in the healing miracle we cannot tell whether the woman approaches Jesus out of superstition, desperation, or true belief in him. It is interesting, though, that Matthew and Luke add the detail of the woman touching the fringe of Christ's garments (Matthew 9:20; Luke 8:44). This is a reference to the 'tassels of remembrance' (Numbers 15:38–40) which Moses had to tell the people to put on the corners of their garments (probably their cloaks) as a reminder of God's commandments. Might it be that the woman is reaching out to a symbol of the old covenant, only to find herself receiving the healing and salvation of the new covenant?

The woman's conviction that she would be healed is stressed in her reported thoughts: 'If I touch even his garments, I shall be made well' (Mark 5:28) and the healing is indeed immediate. Jesus, however, is concerned for her spiritual wellbeing as much as for her physical state. She could not be allowed to creep away without knowing for certain that this was no magical power, possibly a power that was all in her mind, whose healing effects may or may not be lasting. That it is not, is evident by Jesus being drained of his power, and by his certainty that it was more than the crowd knocking against him. So it is out of a desire to save the woman rather than to humiliate her that Jesus calls out to her. As C. E. B. Cranfield puts it, he had to draw her imperfect faith 'away from his clothes to himself'.[1] Luke (8:47) adds the detail that, contrary to her expectations, the woman 'saw that she could not remain hidden'. Her consequent fear may be attributed to many causes: dismay at being found out, the possible anger of Jesus, the sheer emotional and physical suffering she had endured, or, perhaps most likely of all, the overwhelming realization that she was the object of a miracle.

Her fears, once she has told Jesus everything, are relieved in the most compassionate way, as Jesus addresses her affectionately, 'Daughter', and she hears in his words what her body already knows to be the case. But now she learns that this is more than physical healing. Jesus uses the Greek verb *sozein,* meaning both physically 'made well' and also spiritually 'saved'. Significantly the illness which had prevented her from observing her Jewish faith is lifted, but in the process she has been offered instead the wholeness and salvation given by God through his Son.

The context of this miracle is important, coming as it does in the middle of the story of the raising to life of Jairus' daughter. On one level it is the event which causes

Jesus' delay in going to Jairus' house, with the result that
when he arrives the girl is already dead. But on another
level it demonstrates how Jesus' saving power is available
to women as well as men, to the powerful like Jairus and
to the destitute like this unnamed woman of faith.

The Canaanite Woman and her Daughter (Mark 7:24 –30; Matthew 15:22–8)

The setting for this healing miracle is at the northern limits
of Israelite settlements, and is in fact Gentile territory.
Mark describes Jesus as trying to hide away there, but even
here people in great need search him out.

The story is generally interpreted as an indication that
Jesus' ministry, at least before the crucifixion, was for the
Jews and not for Gentiles. In Mark this is expressed only
in his image of the children being fed first, though Matthew
is more explicit: 'I was sent only to the lost sheep of the
house of Israel' (15:24). Yet this is no allegory; rather it is
the report of a healing miracle which owes its impact to
the woman herself and to Jesus' compassionate admiration
for her.

Like the woman with the haemorrhage, this anonymous
woman is desperate. It is the suffering of her 'severely
possessed' daughter that drives her, and keeps driving her
in the face of Jesus' silence and the disciples' attempts,
in Matthew, to get rid of her. Her desperation is further
compounded by the fact that she is utterly convinced that
Jesus has the power to heal the girl, and it is this faith
which gives her the words to counter Jesus' arguments and
which he finally rewards with healing.

The woman's approach to Jesus is respectful. Although
some commentators have suggested that the title 'Son of
David' which Matthew has her use might be applied to
any Jew by a non-Jew, the 'Lord' with which she addresses

Jesus in Mark can only be an expression of reverence, even though the woman does not share his faith.

Jesus' answer to her plea uses the word 'dogs', and although this was and is the supreme insult in Middle Eastern and Eastern cultures, it seems to have been a standard term used by Jews of Gentiles. In any case, it offers a good picture, for no one would snatch children's bread (in other words, their salvation) away from them and throw it to the dogs. But the quick-thinking woman responds with an even better image of her own. Children at table cannot help getting crumbs on the floor, and the dogs under the table are eager to eat them up. It is a clever reply, and the image itself reflects the woman's desperation to get just a crumb of that healing for her daughter. And because of the faith in Christ's power that she reveals, she is rewarded.

Mark's Gospel is not without hope that the Gentiles will eventually receive salvation themselves. 'Let the children be fed first,' says Jesus, suggesting that the turn of others will come. But the woman is not content to wait that long – her daughter's need is far too pressing. So as with Hagar we see here above all the suffering of a mother. But like the woman with the flow of blood, faith saves her, not this time for her own healing but for the healing of her beloved child. And this casting out of evil from a single Gentile girl offers her whole race a foretaste of what lies ahead.

Sharing the Suffering of Christ: Julian of Norwich (1342–1416)

Unlike the suffering of biblical women in its various forms, it might be said that Julian of Norwich's suffering was in a sense self-inflicted. But the outcome of a period of brief but life-threatening illness was one which was to have a profound influence both on people of her own time and those who have rediscovered her *Revelations of Divine Love* much more recently.

Julian, sometimes called Juliana, was thirty years old when in May 1373 she received the 'Revelations' which were to change the course of her life. It is not recorded whether at this time she was already living a life of seclusion as an anchoress, although this is how she was subsequently known. Anchoresses were to be found in many major towns in the fourteenth century and were perceived as the local holy women. Their main calling was to a life of prayer, although they often combined this with other occupations such as craftwork or instructing young girls. The anchorages in which they lived seem to have been comfortable and spacious – not penitential cells – and they were allowed to receive gifts of food and clothing so long as these were compatible with a simple lifestyle. However, Julian stands out from her contemporaries by virtue of her revelatory experience and by her subsequent writing about it, albeit some ten to fifteen years later. In the words of one medieval historian, hers was 'the first major English example of a female vision for two centuries: the same centuries which on the Continent constituted a golden age of women's mysticism'.[2]

After her 'Revelations' Julian lived in an anchorage in a church belonging to a Benedictine community and became known as the 'recluse ate Norwyche'. She gained a reputation as a spiritual adviser, and Margery Kempe (see Chapter 4) was among those who sought her out for this purpose. The two women probably had much in common. Both were concerned that the charge of Lollardy ('babbling') might be levelled against them, and both were anxious to portray themselves with humility. Julian refers to herself at the outset as 'a simple and educated creature', and later she writes:

The fact that I have had this revelation does not mean that I am good. I am good only in so far as I love God the better ... When I look at myself in particular I am obviously of no account; but by and large I am hopeful, for I am united in love with all my fellow Christians.[3]

Futhermore, Julian was scrupulous in submitting her experiences and her interpretation of them to the church, and there is little in them which does not conform to orthodox belief. She is noted nowadays for emphasizing the female and maternal aspects of God and referring to God as 'Mother', although this is well grounded in Scripture. She is less orthodox though in some of her comments on sin, stating that although we are sinners there remains part of us that reflects something of the divine:

In every soul to be saved is a godly will that has never consented to sin, in the past or in the future. Just as there is an animal will in our lower nature that does not will what is good, so there is a godly will in our higher part, which by its basic goodness never wills what is evil, but only what is good. (118)

Julian's translator queries whether this is conscious heresy, or whether it is simply that Julian, accustomed since childhood to being surrounded by happy, loving people, is incapable of seeing deliberate evil in others and seeks a more positive explanation of sin (38).

Julian's period of intense physical suffering is for her an answer to prayer. Some time previously she had asked that she might see for herself the suffering of Jesus on the cross and of those closest to him, the better to understand his passion. She had also prayed that she herself might be 'ill to the point of death' in order to 'undergo all those spiritual and physical sufferings I should have were I really dying,

and to know ... the terror and assaults of the demons'
(63). Finally, she prayed for three 'wounds': the wounds
of true contrition, genuine compassion and sincere longing
for God.

The response to these prayers took the form of an illness
which lasted for about a week and which was so severe
that Julian was given the last rites. Paralysis affected her
lower body and began to creep upwards to affect her
breathing. With her eyesight failing she gazed on a crucifix,
expecting to die at any moment, when suddenly all her
pain was lifted. Having been so close to death she prayed
to suffer with her Lord, and it was then that she received
sixteen revelations. Those concerning Christ's physical suffering are concisely and beautifully reported. Others are
treated more didactically, as Julian goes on to comment at
some length on such subjects as the greatness and goodness
of God, the importance of prayer and the nature of the
Trinity. The *Revelations* as we now have them end with a
statement of her purpose (Julian had by then replaced her
original account with a longer version). This is revealed
to her through her 'spirit's understanding' as a series of
questions and answers:

> You would know our Lord's meaning in this thing?
> Know it well. Love was his meaning. Who showed it
> you? Love. What did he show you? Love. Why did he
> show it? For love. Hold on to this and you will know
> and understand love more and more. (211–12)

It is the passages on suffering, as revealed to a woman
who now understands the nature of pain and the fear of
death, which are the most memorable. To some extent
these reflect a preoccupation with the appearance of
Christ's body on the cross which is frequently found in
medieval art and popular piety. Yet physical suffering is

represented in a way which, far from being sensational, brings home to the reader the full horror of the crucifixion. First there are the effects of Christ's torture:

> I saw insults and spittle and disfiguring and bruising, and lingering pain more than I know how to describe. (76)

Then there is the protracted agony of the cross itself:

> Because of the pull of the nails and the weight of that blessed body it was a long time suffering. For I could see that the great, hard, hurtful nails in those dear and tender hands and feet caused the wounds to gape wide and the body to sag forward under its own weight, and because of the time it hung there. His head was scarred and torn, and the crown was sticking to it, congealed with blood; his dear hair and his withered flesh was entangled with the thorns, and they with it. (89)

And lastly there is the agony of physical thirst: 'there was no comfort to relieve all his suffering and discomfort' (90).

It has to be remembered that Julian's suffering had by now already been taken away from her and she reflects somewhat guiltily: 'All the while he was suffering I personally felt no pain for him' (90). But then she realizes that her own pain has passed beyond physical death:

> Hell is a different pain, for there there is despair as well. But of all the pains that lead to salvation this is the greatest, to see your Love suffer. How could there be greater pain than to see him suffer, who is all my life, my bliss, my joy? Here it was that I truly felt I loved Christ so much more than myself and that there could

be no pain comparable to the sorrow caused by seeing him in pain. (90)

With her vision of Christ's suffering Julian gains understanding and insight into the true meaning of Christ's love. So her message is one of hope: 'In exchange for the little we have to suffer here, we shall have the supreme unending knowledge of God which we should never have without it. The sharper our suffering with him on his cross, the greater our glory with him in his kingdom' (96). Julian's own suffering may have been short, but through it she has brought comfort and inspiration to many Christians, both of her time and of ours.

Simone Weil and 'total affliction'

The French philosopher Simone Weil (1909–43) experienced many forms of suffering in her short life. She was rarely free from physical pain – indeed as a child she was so sickly that she was not expected to survive into adulthood. Perhaps because of that, and also because of her radical left-wing views, she felt an extraordinary affinity for those around her, especially the working classes, whose everyday suffering she witnessed at first hand. This led to her own mental anguish on their account and a desire to share their pain. Nor does her suffering seem to have been confined to that of the body and the mind; her writings on spirituality suggest a spiritual battle which gave her a rare insight into the place of suffering in Christianity.

Simone was born into a Jewish family in Paris, where her father was a doctor. Although she showed signs of considerable intelligence at an early age, she always saw herself as overshadowed by her older brother Andre, who displayed a precocious talent for mathematics. Because of her fragile health, Simone had a succession of home tutors;

when finally she was able to join her contemporaries in public education, first at the prestigious Lycee Henri IV and then at the Ecole Normale Superieure, she excelled in philosophy. Despite her apparently sheltered upbringing, by her late teens Simone was already engaged in left-wing politics and showing a deep concern for human rights. In 1926 she read of the famine which was gripping China and burst into tears. One of her philosophy tutors, Simone de Beauvoir, wrote: 'Her tears more than her talent for philosophy forced me to respect her.'[4] A few years later, in 1930, shortly before completing her studies, Simone began to suffer from incapacitating migraines which were to dog her for the rest of her life.

For the next few years Simone taught philosophy in a succession of girls' schools while becoming increasingly active in trade union matters. In 1934 she took a year off from teaching to undertake unskilled factory work. For someone in uncertain health this was to prove extraordinarily demanding and she was not helped by a lack of manual dexterity which might have been the result of childhood illness or simply the consequence of having unusually small hands. In addition, as she wrote to a former pupil, 'life in the factory involves a perpetual humiliating subordination, for ever at the orders of foremen'.[5] Yet she did not regret her move, in spite of the physical pain caused her by working among noisy machines. In April 1935 she wrote (to Boris Souvarine):

You must wonder how I resist the temptation to back out, since no necessity compels me to suffer these things. I will explain: it is because I scarcely feel any temptation, even at the moments when I am really at the limit of my endurance. Because I don't feel the suffering as mine, I feel it as the workers' suffering; and whether I personally suffer it or not seems to me a detail of almost no importance. Thus the desire to know and understand easily prevails. (18)

In another letter she described how her self-respect had been destroyed by what she called 'brutal constraint', which led her to adopt 'the resigned docility of a beast of burden' – quite a transformation from the rebellious and outspoken teenager she had once been.

Simone did not share the faith of her Jewish family. Her guiding philosophy seems initially to have been a kind of stoicism, coupled with a belief in the beauty and integrity of creation. Yet shortly before the outbreak of war, Simone's thoughts turned to God, inspired at least in part by reading George Herbert's poem 'Love'. In a letter written in 1942 she described it like this:

> During all this time [of her own physical suffering and seeing the suffering of workers around her] the word God had no place at all in my thoughts. It never had, until the day – about three and a half years ago – when I could no longer keep it out. At a moment of intense physical pain, while I was making the effort to love, I felt, while completely unprepared for it (I had never read the mystics), a presence more personal, more certain, and more real than that of a human being; it was inaccessible both to sense and to imagination, and it resembled the love that irradiates the tenderest smile of someone who loves. Since that moment, the name of God and the name of Christ have been more and more irresistibly mingled with my thoughts. (140)

Although never received into the Christian church, Simone wrote, in the same year:

I adhere totally to the mysteries of the Christian faith, with the only kind of adherence which seems to me appropriate for mysteries. This adherence is love, not affirmation. Certainly I belong to Christ – or so I hope and believe. (155)

When France was occupied in 1940, Simone's parents first sought refuge in the unoccupied south, before leaving for the United States. Simone went with them, but immediately began to look for work in London with the Free French. She was particularly attracted by espionage work, and was very disappointed simply to be offered a desk job. Her argument for a more dangerous occupation was ingenious: her factory work had already shown her what it meant to lose one's self-respect – so she would by an effort of will thwart the enemy's attempts to wear her down by getting herself to that state already. Furthermore, her natural physical weakness would quickly bring her to a point where her mind was a blank and she would not be able to give anything away. She was also anxious to share in what she perceived as the world's suffering:

The suffering all over the world obsesses and overwhelms me to the point of annihilating my faculties and the only way I can revive them and release myself from the obsession is by getting for myself a large share of danger and hardship. That is a necessary condition before I can exert my capacity for work. (156)

But Simone never had this opportunity. In London in 1943 she was again ill, but this time her illness was made worse by her refusal to be treated any better than her compatriots back in France, nor would she accept help from the English: 'I cannot eat the bread of the English without taking part in their war effort' (178).

In August 1943 Simone Weil died in Ashford in Kent from a lung infection complicated by malnutrition. It has to be said that those treating her seem to have regarded her with suspicion, if not contempt, assuming that she was trying to commit suicide. In reality, it was her physical weakness combined with high moral principles which led to her death, bringing to an end thirty-four years of almost continual suffering.

Some of Simone's insights into suffering and the Christian faith are set out in an essay written a few days before she left for the United States in May 1942, published with the title 'L'Amour de Dieu et le Malheur' ('Love of God and Affliction').[6] These 'unordered thoughts', as the original French editor termed them, were sent to a Dominican, Pere Perrin. Simone begins by defining *malheur* as something which is not physical suffering: it is distinct from it yet also inseparable from it; it 'takes over and enslaves the soul'. Prolonged or frequent suffering may also lead to *malheur* which is a lesser version of death, an uprooting of life. In this extreme affliction thought is no longer possible. *Malheur* is what drove Christ to beg to be spared the cross and to utter his cry of dereliction from it. It is the absence of God, when the soul is submerged in sorrow. The soul is pierced by a physical manifestation of the infinite distance which separates God and his creation – a powerful interpretation of Christ's words from the cross. For Simone Weil, it is knowledge of this state of 'total affliction' which is the key to Christian belief.

Simone Weil's interpretation of suffering is rooted in her own lifelong experience of pain. She goes beyond the mystics in their longing to know Christ's sufferings for themselves in that she submits to sharing the pain of others as well as her own, until she understands his 'total affliction' for herself.

6

Women of Faith

> Faith is the assurance of things hoped for, the conviction of things not seen. (Hebrews 11:1)

The pages of Scripture are full of examples of women of great faith. It could also be said that most of the other women featured in this book also deserve that title. This chapter features two of the greatest of such women in the Bible, together with women from both the Old and New Testaments whose faith has been expressed without words. Then there are two famous names from later history. These women must serve as representatives of countless others.

Hannah (1 Samuel 1–2:21)

When Eli the priest came across Hannah in the House of the Lord at Shiloh, she was 'pouring out [her] soul before the Lord' (1 Samuel 1:15). She could not have been a very impressive figure, red-eyed, unable to eat and apparently moaning to herself. Eli thought she was drunk. He could hardly have got things more wrong.

Certainly Hannah was suffering. She suffered from the taunts of her husband's other wife, Peninnah, who always chose the emotive time of the family's annual pilgrimage to Shiloh to mock Hannah's lack of children, taken to indicate God's disfavour with her. Hannah also suffered from a lack of understanding on the part of her husband.

Although Elkanah clearly loves and prefers her, he is unable to put himself in her place. He himself has no troubles – he has children by Peninnah – and even though he is part of the society which stigmatizes barrenness, he believes that Hannah should be satisfied with what she has: 'Am I not more to you than ten sons?' (1:8). In her misery, Hannah turns to God and bargains with him. If God answers her prayer for a son, she will 'set him before you as a nazirite until the day of his death' (1:11).

As is seen in Hannah's further promise that the son's hair shall not be cut, and as the NRSV makes explicit, she is offering her child as a kind of lay minister. The details of this ministry, which was open to both men and women, are set out in Numbers 6. For a given period the nazirites set themselves apart for God, and during this time they abstained from alcohol, kept their hair uncut, and stayed well clear of any dead bodies which would make them unclean. In Judges 13, the wife of Manoah is promised a son on condition that he becomes a nazirite not for a limited period but for his whole life. In this case, the son, Samson, received extraordinary strength as well, until his hair was cut off and his 'separation for God' came to a sudden and horrific end. Even so, the faith of Samson's mother was rewarded by a son who later came to be listed as one of the heroes of faith (Hebrews 11:32). Perhaps Samson was in Hannah's mind, for she spontaneously promises more than was necessary for a nazirite – that he would be set apart for God as long as he lived.

Although Eli's conversation with Hannah gets off to a bad start, he is quickly convinced of her faith and blesses her: 'Go in peace; the God of Israel grant the petition you have made to him' (1:17). That is enough for Hannah. She recognizes God's answer to her prayer, and when her son is born she (not her husband) calls him Samuel, variously interpreted as meaning 'God gives' or 'heard of God'.

Hannah's faith and her faithfulness to her side of the bargain do not waver. After Samuel's birth it is striking that, with her husband's consent, she does not join the annual pilgrimage to Shiloh, until the time, presumably two or three years later, when she will hand her boy over for good. This makes the day when her vow is honoured all the more special, although it is also tempting to think that Hannah would have particularly valued this time or times alone with her son.

When the day comes, it is indeed a momentous occasion, marked by sizable gifts of a bull, wine and flour. Hannah reminds Eli of their previous meeting: 'I am the woman who was standing here in your presence, praying to the Lord. For this child I prayed' (1:26–7). This emphasis on prayer is taken up in the song with which Hannah closes the episode. This, however, is not quite the end of the story. Hannah is a faithful mother as well as a faithful woman of prayer, and in 1 Samuel 2 we are given the touching detail that 'His mother used to make for him a little robe and take it to him each year, when she went up with her husband to offer the yearly sacrifice, (2:19). This does not go unnoticed by Eli and his response is to offer Elkanah and Hannah far more than Hannah originally prayed for: 'May the Lord repay you with children by this woman for the gift that she made to the Lord' (2:17). This prayer is abundantly answered with the couple having no fewer than three sons and two daughters. Meanwhile, 'Samuel continued to grow both in stature and in favour with the Lord and with the people' (2:26), a verse which has clear echoes in Luke 2:52 relating to the boy Jesus.

It has been suggested that Hannah's song marks her out as a prophetess. Like Mary's song it celebrates the power of God particularly in reversing situations – the hungry are fed and the well-fed have to look for food. However, the personal element which is so marked at the beginning of the Magnificat is here rather more general and stylized. 'My mouth derides my enemies because I rejoice in my victory' (2:1). This may be a reference to Hannah's suffering at the hands of Peninnah, but otherwise the focus is wholly on God. Nonetheless, the lines 'The barren has borne seven, but she who has many children is forlorn' (2:5), though not a fully accurate prophecy in her own case, are poignant.

In keeping with her predominantly prophetic tone, Hannah also delivers a warning: 'Talk no more so very proudly, let not arrogance come from your mouth, for the Lord is a God of knowledge, and by him actions are weighed' (2:3). Certainly this proved to be Hannah's own experience, which is overwhelmingly that of faith rewarded.

Rizpah's Silent Vigil (2 Samuel 21: 1–4)

Like a number of other biblical women, Rizpah – one of Saul's concubines and mother of two of his sons – was a victim of history and of factors beyond her control. The part of Israel's history that she found herself sucked into had to do with the relationship between Israel and the Gibeonites, whose story is begun in Joshua 9. Briefly, the Gibeonites had deceived Israel's leaders into believing they had travelled from a distant land (although they were in fact defecting from the Amorites, with whom Israel and Judah were at war) and as a result Joshua made a covenant with them to spare their lives (Joshua 9:15). The Gibeonites were soon found out, but too late – all Joshua could do was to relegate them to the level of slaves, making them 'hewers of wood and drawers of water for all the congregation' (9:21). So the Gibeonites remained in Israel and much later are recorded as helping Nehemiah rebuild the walls of Jerusalem (Nehemiah 3:7).

Some two hundred years on, King Saul was not interested in peaceful co-existence. Possibly mindful of Joshua's
significant omission in not seeking God's will before saving
the Gibeonites, he broke the covenant promise and slaugh-
tered an unspecified number of them (2 Samuel 21:1), 'in
his zeal for the people of Israel and Judah' (21:2). After
Saul's death God punished this act with a three-year famine
and it fell to David to put things right, so that the Gibeonites might 'bless the heritage of the Lord' (21:3). The Gibeonites' quarrel was not with David or Israel but with Saul
himself, so in retribution they demanded the death of seven
of Saul's sons, among them the two sons of Rizpah, and
the men were duly hanged.

Rizpah's reaction to this horrific event comes not in
words but in a bold and silent vigil. As the dead king's
concubine she would have enjoyed a certain status; yet, as
2 Samuel 21 tells us, she 'took sackcloth and spread it on
a rock for herself' (21:10), alone on the mountain on which
her sons lay dead – an act of considerable bravery on
her part. It is more than an expression of maternal grief,
although no doubt that was what motivated her. Hers was,
perhaps, the first recorded act of silent protest. After her
sons' death, the justification of which lay deep in history,
Rizpah was denied the opportunity to give them a proper
burial, something which was of great significance in Jewish
culture.

So Rizpah waited, alone, in mourning, and probably in
extreme anguish and discomfort, faithfully watching over
the bodies of her sons. And all the time she was waiting,
God showed no sign of alleviating the famine: it was the
beginning of the harvest season but there had been no rain.
David, though, understood her silent message. He himself
went to gather up the unburied bones of Saul and Jonathan
and also those of the seven sons of Israel, and had them
properly buried. Only then, when Rizpah was giving up

her vigil, did God heed 'supplications for the land' (21:14) and the rain came.

There was no possibility that Rizpah could have prevented her sons' death. However, by her silent protest she was able to secure their burial; and David's response, which rectified Saul's misdeeds and enabled the Amorites and Israelites to be reconciled, was honoured by God. So the bumpy course of Israel's history was for the time being smoothed over, thanks to the powerful, wordless action of Rizpah, the mother faithfully grieving for her innocent sons.

Mary the Mother of Jesus (Luke 1:26–36)

Although Mary perhaps most immediately commands attention as a woman giving life (and she will be considered as such in Chapter 10), the circumstances which led to her giving birth to the Son of God, what little we know of her life thereafter, and above all the link between her song in Luke 1 and the song of Hannah, all suggest that she also has a special place among women of faith.

It is not through any human estimation of Mary's worth but from the messenger of God himself that we learn of this young girl's outstanding qualities. She has found favour with God, says Gabriel; and this is much more than God looking kindly on a faithful Jewish girl. Gabriel comes to her to say, 'The Lord is with you!' And there is more to come: 'The Holy Spirit will come upon you and the power of the Most High will overshadow you' (Luke 1:35). Those who regard Mary as the bearer – the ark – of the new covenant, will see here a parallel with Exodus 40:35, where the glory of the Lord fills the tabernacle housing the ark of the (old) covenant. This is not language to be used simply of devout Jews. The faithfulness of Mary is such that God responds to it in a hitherto unimaginable way.

Mary's feelings, even distress, at Gabriel's appearance

are hardly surprising, although once the angel has explained himself her dismay turns to surprise and practical questions. She knows it is not possible for her to have conceived by human means. Interestingly, it may be the detail of Elizabeth's already advanced pregnancy, something she would have known to be out of the question, that convinces Mary of the truth of Gabriel's message and demonstrates clearly to her that 'nothing will be impossible with God'. And it is this conversation with the angel that prompts one of the greatest declarations of faith in all Scripture: 'Here am I, the servant of the Lord; let it be with me according to your word' (Luke 1:38). To be sure these are hardly eloquent, or even novel, words (reminiscent perhaps of the young Samuel's obedient response, 'Speak, for your servant is listening', 1 Samuel 3:10). But given Mary's present situation, what has just happened to her and what is to befall her in the future, they form a momentous statement which heralds a new era in human history. For with Mary's simple acceptance of God's will, the new age of the Messiah surely begins to dawn.

A further key statement of Mary's faith is expressed when Mary visits Elizabeth. There she not only sees for herself the truth of Gabriel's words about her pregnancy, but in the response of Elizabeth and her unborn child to her presence she also receives human confirmation of Gabriel's promise about the future greatness of her own son. Elizabeth addresses her as 'the mother of my Lord', yet her tribute to Mary is above all a tribute to her faith: 'Blessed is she who believed there would be a fulfilment of what was spoken to her by the Lord' (Luke 1:45).

Mary's reply to these words, which also of course illustrate Elizabeth's own faith, is a statement of faith in itself. The Magnificat (Luke 1:46–55) has a style of ancient prophecy about it, proclaiming God's promises to his people and celebrating his glory. This 'glorious song of spiritual praise and prophetic worship'[1] also echoes the songs of Hannah and Deborah as well as the short burst of praise from Miriam (Exodus 15:21). Still greater demands will be placed on Mary's faith, though, than was the case with her Old Testament predecessors.

The depth of Mary's faith is evident in the way in which she describes herself: she is humble, yet 'the Mighty One has done great things for me' – on the face of it an extraordinary statement, given that in a few months' time Mary will be returning home to face those who will see her condition as utterly shameful. And this is no assumed humility. Later, when Mary and Joseph take Jesus to be circumcised, the sacrifice they make is that prescribed for poorer women.[2] From a personal song of praise Mary then turns to the powerful acts of God on behalf of his people in the past and her anticipation of what is to come:

He has brought down the powerful from their thrones
and has lifted up the lowly;
he has filled the hungry with good things,
and has sent the rich away empty. (Luke 1:52–3)

The past tense in these verses is prophetic: the speaker is so certain the events will take place and has such a vivid image of them that she relates them as if they had already happened. They are closely modelled on Hannah's song, with its general statement of God's power:

The Lord makes poor and makes rich;
He brings low, he also exalts. (1 Samuel 2:7)

In Mary's song, though, this becomes a promise of a new order for the poor and hungry which will find its fulfilment in the person of her son. There is also an echo of Isaiah 61 which will be read by Jesus in the synagogue in

Nazareth and applied to himself: 'He has anointed me to preach good news to the poor' (Luke 4:18f.). And this anticipates Jesus' teaching in the Sermon on the Mount, with its promise of blessings for the poor, the hungry, the sad and the rejected and woes to the rich and well fed.

Faith is rarely comfortable: it demands courage. And just as Abraham set out in faith, so from the moment of Gabriel's annunciation Mary also sets out on the first of many journeys of faith. After the visit to Elizabeth comes a complete break with her past, as she embarks on a life as mother and wife. Then there is the difficult journey to Bethlehem, followed all too soon by the life of a refugee in Egypt, to save her newborn son. And if Jesus' upbringing shows him growing in wisdom, then surely this was also for Mary a journey of discovery as she gradually learns more about her son. This must have been an increasingly difficult and perplexing progression as Jesus begins a ministry which was to be widely misunderstood, taking him to the cross.

We shall be looking at Mary as mother later on, but it is worth remembering that she is also a faithful disciple. Her presence among the disciples before Pentecost is testimony to her great and lasting faith: 'All these were constantly devoting themselves to prayer, together with certain women, including Mary the mother of Jesus, as well as his brothers' (Acts 1:14). It is fitting that this final detail of Mary's life in the New Testament should show her in the same attitude as when we first meet her: at prayer and in the presence of God.

The Silent Faith of Jesus' Followers

> Standing near the cross of Jesus were his mother, and his mother's sister, Mary the wife of Clopas, and Mary Magdalene. (John 19:25)

There is a small but highly significant group of women in the New Testament who, when the spotlight is turned on them, are completely silent. This is not because they have nothing to say: quite the reverse – they have an important message. But it is one that is conveyed not so much through words as through silent action or even, in the case of the women at the foot of the cross, simply silent presence. In all four Gospels we find women of faith whose main concern is silently to serve Jesus. Depending on circumstances, their acts of service may entail sacrifice, the risk of being misunderstood or even of physical danger.

The Woman with the Alabaster Jar (Luke 7:36–50)

Unlike other women who serve Jesus, the person whose story is told in Luke 7 acts completely on her own. Confusingly, her action in anointing Jesus' feet and wiping them with her hair, is the same as that performed by Mary of Bethany (John 12:1–8) on the day before Jesus entered Jerusalem. Yet modern commentators tend to agree that the woman in Luke is different: the event happens much earlier in Jesus' ministry and the woman is described as 'a sinner', which seems hardly to fit the sister of Lazarus. Nor are there any good grounds for following popular tradition and identifying her with Mary of Magdala. In Luke's account the woman who carries out this striking act of service neither speaks nor has a name.

The woman's action is disturbing for several reasons. To those watching it was shocking that Jesus should allow himself to become ceremonially unclean by letting a woman with a bad reputation touch him. Equally shocking is that this unlikely woman serves as a rebuke to Jesus' host, Simon the Pharisee, for we are soon told that Simon had not offered his guest such generous anointing – he had not even given him water for his feet or a kiss of greeting.

But surely most shocking of all is the intimate nature of what the woman does: her action as she caresses Jesus' feet with her hair and then her lips is without parallel in the Gospels.

Only Jesus speaks in this encounter, so the silent woman's feelings have to be deduced from her weeping and her behaviour towards Jesus. Whatever she may have done in the past, her immediate reaction is penitence, expressed in her tears. And that release of her emotions turns to gratitude as she serves Jesus more lovingly and more generously than Simon could ever have done.

So, without a word, Jesus accepts her silent service. Then he deflects Simon's unspoken rebuke to them both ('If this man were a prophet, he would have known . . . what kind of woman this is' (7:39), with the example of two creditors, and turns it into a reproach of Simon himself. Only then does he tell the woman, 'Your sins are forgiven . . . Your faith has saved you; go in peace' (7:48, 50).

We are not told what prompted the woman to act in the first place. G. B. Caird[3] suggests that her heart had been softened simply by listening to Jesus. In expressing her tearful penitence she braves the scorn and abuse of the Pharisee and those present in his house, although in the event it is Jesus who articulates Simon's unspoken thoughts (7:47). The woman's courage, her humility and her generosity contrasts strikingly with others closer to Jesus, not least the disciples who were to argue about which of them was the greatest and who would run away from Gethsemane. Jesus acknowledges this: 'she has shown great love', although it is her faith that saves her – a faith which lies in recognizing who Jesus is and behaving accordingly in response, without any need for words.

The Women at the Cross

It is a natural step for Luke to move from his story of one woman's service to an acknowledgement that many women served Jesus. At the beginning of chapter 8 he singles out three women who had been healed and who were among the travelling group of disciples: Mary of Magdala, Joanna wife of Chuza, and Susanna. Then there is his recognition of 'many others, who provided for them out of their resources' (8:3). So silently, often anonymously, women were alongside Jesus, faithfully serving him as disciples or giving material support.

We meet this silent service once more in the Gospels: at the cross. When the male disciples had long since gone to ground, except for the Beloved Disciple who remained there until Jesus told him to take his mother away, the women stayed. John's Gospel names three Marys as standing 'near' the cross (19:25); Matthew (27:55) and Mark (15:40) speak of a group of women, some of whom are named and others who are not, 'looking on from a distance', disciples who had accompanied Jesus from Galilee and ministered to him.

A Scandinavian Noblewoman: St Bridget of Sweden (c. 1302–73)

> Her greatest legacy ... comes with those twenty and more years of waiting, and then afterwards with the answer that appeared to run counter to everything she had given her life to. The twinned experiences of waiting and failure make her more genuinely relevant to the lives of ordinary Christians ... than anything else in her story.[4]

Bridget was the eldest daughter of a powerful Swedish judge who was also a great landowner. She was brought up to the north-east of Stockholm and already as a child experienced visions, including one of Christ on the cross. However, her life was not yet to be spent in religious devotion. When she was thirteen her marriage was arranged to Ulf Gudmarsson, also a wealthy judge, and for the next twenty-seven years Bridget was a dutiful wife and mother. She was also very rich, having inherited seven estates from her mother, in addition to her husband's wealth, and she enjoyed a position of influence at the Swedish court. She gave birth to eight children, five of whom survived.

Bridget's family and busy social life did not, however, suppress her natural spirituality. She was a considerable influence on her husband in spiritual matters and acquired a reputation as a gifted spiritual adviser. In 1341, probably when their children were more independent, Bridget and Ulf went together on a pilgrimage to Santiago de Compostela. As a result they adopted a life of chastity and abstinence and planned to enter a monastery, but Ulf died a couple of years later before their plan could become a reality.

It was after Ulf's death that Bridget once again began to experience visions. In the first of many 'revelations' God called her to a new ministry. From then on her task would be to found a new religious order and to work for the spiritual renewal of the secular and religious leaders of her day. So far from living a secluded life of prayer in the monastery to which she had withdrawn when her husband died, Bridget found her future taking a very different direction.

During the 1340s Bridget took an increasingly active role in public affairs. She was free with her advice to the King of Sweden, urging him to rule with moderation and charity, and to give to the poor one-tenth of all the money coming into the treasury. She also addressed what she saw as social injustice. One cause she took up was the custom that ships wrecked off the Swedish coast should become the property of the local inhabitants. She was eloquent in her condemnation:

> Oh! What inhuman cruelty to increase the misery of those already in distress. Is it not sufficient grief for the afflicted to have lost their ship? Shall they also lose their other possessions?[5]

In 1348 Bridget made a personal appeal to Pope Clement VI, then in residence in Avignon, to return to Rome to reform the church. In her letter, which she wrote according to Christ's instructions, she warned of judgement to come – and this was of course the year of the Black Death in Europe. She also sent a delegation from the Swedish King to the Kings of France and Italy, encouraging them to make peace. This was a matter close to Bridget's heart, as she had seen the misery caused by the war when she travelled through France to Spain on her pilgrimage a few years before.

By then people were becoming increasingly uneasy at Bridget's activities. She had asked the King to lead a Crusade, and in 1348 he set out against the non-Christian Karelia, only to lose the territory altogether. However, Bridget was now called to a new mission. In 1349 she set out for Rome, as Clement, although still in Avignon, had proclaimed 1350 a Holy Year. She was commanded to stay in Rome until the Pope returned, and thus began her patient twenty-year wait. So Bridget found herself far from her native land and in surroundings which could hardly have been more different from the peace of a Swedish monastery which she had originally instinctively sought. In Rome she lived as a private citizen, spending much of her time in prayer and fasting, with occasional pilgrimages to Assisi and other centres. But she had not forgotten her call to found a new order. She evolved a rule of life for herself which was to be the order's model, and sought divine guidance on the practical details.

One such problem was the question of a lectionary: what portions of Scripture should the sisters read? In answer to her prayer, Christ appeared to her with the promise: 'I shall send to thee one of my Angels who will make known to thee the lessons which must be read at Matins by the Sisters of thy monastery, to the honour of the Virgin my Mother.' An angel then dictates instructions to her, although the modern editor of the *Sermo Angelicus* comments that this adds nothing new to Scripture and the tradition of the Catholic Church, a sign perhaps of Bridget's faithfulness to her church's teaching despite the corruption she saw in its establishment. At the end of his dictation, the angel says to Bridget:

> Behold I have now cut the cloth to make a tunic for the Mother of God, the Queen of heaven; do thou now sew it together as best thou canst.[6]

When Bridget's period of faithful waiting finally came to an end, there was little satisfaction in it for her. Pope Urban V came to Rome in 1367, but stayed only two years before going back to Avignon. To make matters worse, he approved the creation of her new order in 1370, but only in a form which was quite different from what she intended. It was much the same as existing institutions which Bridget had long decided were in need of spiritual regeneration.

Bridget's reaction to what was apparently a double failure was to embark on a pilgrimage to the Holy Land in 1372. She still persisted in her attempts to persuade the popes to leave Avignon, but this was to be the last year of her life. At Jerusalem she received a vision of Calvary and by the following summer she was dead.

Bridget's faithfulness was not, however, in vain. In 1378, the beginning of the Great Schism, her followers supported the new Pope in Rome, against the anti-Pope in Avignon, and in return he approved Bridget's order more or less as she had originally intended it to be. Bridget's unswerving loyalty to orthodox belief and her patient faithfulness and obedience to her Lord did not in the end go unrewarded.

'Something Beautiful for God': Mother Teresa of Calcutta (1910–97)

> Lord,
> Increase my faith,
> bless my efforts and work,
> now and for evermore.[7]

The life of Mother Teresa, the Albanian nun whose work among the poorest of the poor in the slums of Calcutta and elsewhere became known around the world, has been well documented. In spite of Mother Teresa's dislike of publicity for the more personal details of her life, there have been a number of biographies, the earliest of which, Malcolm Muggeridge's *Something Beautiful for God*, published in 1971, did much to publicize her cause and resulted in its sceptical author eventually being received into the Roman Catholic Church. Muggeridge wrote of her:

> Words cannot convey how beholden I am to her. She has given me a whole new vision of what being a Christian means; of the amazing power of love, and how in one dedicated soul it can burgeon to cover the whole world.[8]

But although Mother Teresa's work, which was not always free from controversy, was frequently the object of media attention, the faith that throughout her life underpinned everything she did, has tended to receive less comment, at least outside her own church, although she herself was never reticent about her wholehearted trust in God.

Mother Teresa was born Agnes Gonxha Bojaxhiu, the daughter of an Albanian trader living in Skopje, now the capital of Macedonia. Although her father died when she was only seven, she did not forget the unstinting welcome his household unfailingly gave to the local poor. One of his maxims was 'never eat a single mouthful unless you are sharing it with others'.[9]

When she was twelve Agnes experienced a conviction that she was called to the religious life. Six years later she joined the Irish Order of the Sisters of Loreto and took the name Teresa, after the French saint Therese de Lisieux. After only a few weeks of English lessons Teresa was on her way to India, where her languages henceforth were to be English and Bengali. She did not, however, throw in her lot with the poor straightaway, spending the next seventeen years as a teacher at a Calcutta high school for privileged Bengali girls. In 1946, though, she received a further call in which God directed her to leave her comfortable convent life to help the poor while living among them in the slums. She had no doubt that this was God's will for her life: 'It was an order. To fail it would have been to break the faith.'[10]

Teresa's faithfulness to that command was unswerving, although it was not easy. 'There were times . . . when she'd be humiliated, and tears would be streaming down her cheeks. [She] told herself, "I'll teach myself to beg, no matter how much abuse and humiliation I have to endure." '[11] With a dozen sisters, Teresa started her own 'little society' which became the Missionaries of Charity.

With the Vatican's consent she added a further vow to those of poverty, chastity and obedience: 'unremittingly' to seek out the poor, abandoned, sick, infirm and dying. One key aspect of her work was enabling the poor to die with dignity and feeling that they were loved. She would then arrange for the rites of the deceased's own religion to be performed, never imposing her own Catholicism on anyone. But she would tell her sisters, 'I hope and pray you are conscious of your responsibility to the Church. You are the sign of God, the proof of his living love for men.'[12]

In 1979 Mother Teresa received the Nobel Peace Prize, because 'poverty and distress also constitute a threat to peace'. The traditional banquet was cancelled at her request and the US$ 7,000 that it would have cost was given to the poor. In her Prize Lecture she told the distinguished guests: 'Love begins at home, and it is not how much we do, but how much love we put in the action that we do. It is to God almighty . . . how much we do to him in the person that we are serving.'[13]

In the course of her life Mother Teresa created a network of 569 missions serving the poor in 120 different countries. She caused controversy with her fiercely defended conservative views on abortion and birth control, and questions were sometimes asked about the sources of her funding, yet she won the hearts of world leaders, the rich and the famous. She never worried about finding the money for her ever expanding activities: 'The Lord sends it . . . We do his work; he provides the means.'[14]

In 1996, when her health was declining, the sisters finally elected a new leader for their Order. Mother Teresa had tried to retire some six or seven years earlier, but her sisters persuaded her to continue: 'I was expecting to be free,' she said then, 'but God has his own plans. It is God's will and we have to do what he wants from us. God's work will continue with great love.'[15]

In an interview with *Time* magazine on 4 December 1989, Mother Teresa was asked how it felt to be a vehicle of God's grace in the world. She replied: 'It is [God's] work. I think God wants to show his greatness by using nothingness.' She went on to use a memorable image:

> I am like a little pencil in his hand ... He does the thinking. He does the writing. The pencil has nothing to do with it. The pencil has only to be allowed to be used. In human terms the success of our work should not have happened.

Mother Teresa stressed again and again the importance of the poorest people, describing them as God's greatest gift to her because to be with them was to be with Jesus. She would downplay the difficult times and emphasize the joy of the poor when they die in peace.

News of Mother Teresa's death reached the UK on the morning of the funeral of her friend Diana, Princess of Wales – a further shock to a nation already grieving on a scale unprecedented in recent years. Yet it would have been the sorrow of her adopted Indian people that would surely have touched her heart more. A weeping Muslim driver was reported as saying simply of this woman of faith: 'She was a source of perpetual joy.'[16] Her faith, and that of the other women considered in this chapter, may best be summed up in one of her short but memorable prayers:

> Here I am Lord – body, heart and soul.
> Grant that with your love,
> I may be big enough to reach the world,
> And small enough to be at one with you.[17]

*   *   *

The successors to the often silent women of faith in the Bible are in a sense all around us. In so far as she shunned publicity, Mother Teresa herself might have been among them, but for the power of modern media and communications. The silent women are those who are either among the unnamed faithful of history or are people who have simply not wanted their story to be widely known, or cannot imagine it would be of any interest to anyone if it were. They are those to whom in the Sermon on the Mount Jesus promised the Kingdom of Heaven.

Poets and Prophets

> Your sons and your daughters shall prophesy. (Joel 2:28)

> All the singing-men and singing-women have spoken of Josiah in their laments to this day. (2 Chronicles 35:25)

There are two areas of activity in both Old and New Testaments where it seems that women enjoy fully equal standing with men. Both are dependent on God-given gifts: one is the spiritual gift of prophecy and the other appears variously as singing, dancing or poetic composition.

There are of course far fewer women prophets known by name than there are men, at least in the Old Testament. This may be a consequence of the role of a prophet often to be a lone and wandering voice, not an easy place for a woman to be, or the result of culture and education. The classical prophets would often collect associates round them and work as a 'school' of prophecy. Again, this is a way of life which would not have been an option for women, besides demanding learning and perhaps literacy.

It is interesting that the women who do exercise the gift of prophecy in the Old Testament are mostly also notable for other gifts and activities. Deborah was a prophet, but we have already seen too her effectiveness as a judge and military leader. Prophecy and musical composition often seem to go together, and again we have already noted her prophetic songs. The same is true of Miriam and perhaps

Hannah: they are remarkable for other things besides their prophetic utterances.

In the New Testament, where the prophecy of Joel is fulfilled on the Day of Pentecost, there is a marked absence of prophecy in the traditional sense, although men and women alike exercised the gift in the early church. Thus Paul in 1 Corinthians 11 berates equally men who pray or prophesy with something on their heads and women who pray or prophesy with their heads uncovered.

Miriam (Exodus 15:20–2)

Miriam is a prime example of a woman who was known as a prophet and who used music and dance to accompany her prophetic utterances. The context of these few verses in Exodus 15 is important. The Israelites have successfully escaped from the Egyptians who were drowned trying to pursue them through the Red Sea. Most of the chapter is taken up with Moses' song of praise following this miraculous escape: 'I will sing to the Lord, for he has triumphed gloriously' (15:1). This is followed by the short song from Miriam who is accompanied by women with tambourines and dancing. Perhaps this was intended to form a kind of response to Moses, since Miriam simply takes up a couple of lines from his song. We can imagine the prophet leading a lively celebration in answer to the lengthy recital of God's powerful actions on behalf of his people.

The later episode involving Miriam, where she and Aaron criticize Moses for marrying a Cushite (see Chapter 1 above), is fully in keeping with her being a prophetess, even though her intervention on that occasion is shown to be mistaken. She has the courage and ability to stand up to male leaders and to speak out. In all probability she was a natural leader, though we have no further details of her activities. But it is Deborah who epitomizes above all the combination of leadership, prophecy and musical composition in a woman, as we have also already seen in Chapter 1.

Huldar (2 Kings 22:11–20; 2 Chronicles 34:22–8)

The episode in which the prophetess Huldar is sought out by the high priest Hilkiah is an intriguing one. The year is around 621 BC, and King Josiah is on the throne in Jerusalem, following an unhappy period under King Manasseh which was characterized by idol worship and bloodshed. Josiah was an upright man and he set about repairing the Jerusalem Temple. In the course of the work the high priest discovered the book of the law which his scribe then read to the king. Josiah was overwhelmed by its contents and its significance: 'Great is the wrath of the Lord that is kindled against us, because our ancestors did not obey the words of this book' (2 Kings 22:13). Indeed, the threat of punishment had long being hanging over Judah. Back in the reign of Josiah's father, God had announced through unnamed prophets: 'I am bringing upon Jerusalem and Judah such evil that the ears of everyone who hears of it will tingle' (2 Kings 21:12).

On this occasion, though, Josiah appoints a delegation to find out more from the Lord about what he has read in the book. Interestingly they do not approach either Jeremiah or Zephaniah, both of whom were prophesying at the time, but a woman, Huldar. She was certainly close by, being the wife of the 'keeper of the wardrobe', though whether this refers to the royal wardrobe or priestly vestments is not known.

Huldah has two prophecies to offer. The first confirms Josiah's fears. God says, 'I will indeed bring disaster on this place and on its inhabitants' (22:16), a consequence of Judah's worship of other gods. Secondly, though, Huldah has softer words for the godly Josiah. God acknowledges the king's repentance on behalf of his people, and promises him: 'You shall be gathered to your grave in peace; your eyes shall not see all the disaster that I will bring on this place' (22:20). It is not long before both these prophecies are fulfilled, although how peaceful Josiah's death was – he was struck down by an arrow in battle at Megiddo – is debatable.

Huldah then disappears from the story as suddenly as she appeared. When Josiah dies it is Jeremiah who leads the lamentation which is taken up by the male and female singers (2 Chronicles 35:25).

False Prophets

Just as men and women appear to be equal recipients of the gift of prophecy, so too both may qualify as false prophets. This point is made most tellingly in Ezekiel 13. The gist of the criticism is common to men and women alike: they 'prophesy out of their own imagination' (13:2), but this takes a different form in each group.

The men are accused of misleading the people, 'saying, "Peace", when there is no peace' (13:10), and they attribute to God their 'false visions and . . . utter lying divinations' (13:9). The women on the other hand, seem to be engaging in a kind of witchcraft, sewing magic bands on people's wrists. Their purposes are the exact opposite of God's, 'putting to death those who should not die and keeping alive those who should not live' (13:19). They dishearten the righteous falsely in the name of God and encourage the wicked (13:22).

The greater punishment, though, seems to be reserved for the men – perhaps they were more effective. They are threatened with God's wrath and certain death, 'and you shall know that I am the Lord' (13:14). To the false prophetesses God says simply, 'I will save my people from your hand. Then you will know that I am the Lord' (13:27).

Apart from this group of women there is just one woman prophet in the Old Testament who is named yet who seems less than inspired. She is Noadiah (Nehemiah 6:14) who, along with other prophets, tried to instil fear into Nehemiah, presumably to deflect him from his purpose in rebuilding the walls of Jerusalem. Nehemiah prays that God will remember them 'according to these things that they did', in the hope that they will eventually get their just deserts.

So equal opportunities in prophecy also means the licence to be a false prophet or prophetess. Women may be memorable in their success, but no less than men they will attract God's wrath if they abuse their position.

Anna (Luke 2:36–40)

By the time of Jesus, the age of the great prophets was long past, and after Malachi the voice of prophecy had fallen silent. It is only with the events surrounding the birth of Jesus that we are aware of a brief flurry of prophetic activity whose purpose is to announce the coming of the Messiah. The prophet primarily entrusted with this task is, of course, John the Baptist. But this does not mean a total lack of awareness of the Messiah's birth on the part of God-fearing people. It is two elderly people, Simeon and Anna, both of whom have been patiently waiting for the Messiah, who are given prophetic insight when Jesus is brought to the Temple for circumcision.

All we know of Simeon is that he is righteous and devout and 'the Holy Spirit rested on him' (Luke 2:25). Although he is not called a prophet, his words to Mary are truly and richly prophetic. About Anna we are told still less. Like great figures from Israel's history she has lived to a ripe old age, and would have been over a hundred years old when she finally set eyes on the Messiah. Anna, though is clearly designated a prophet. Unlike Simeon she is a constant presence in the Temple, worshipping God through fasting and prayer.

Anna witnessed Simeon taking Jesus into his arms and no doubt heard him acclaim 'a light for revelation to the Gentiles and for glory to . . . Israel' (2:31–2). Perhaps she also overheard his words to Mary, 'This child is destined for the falling and the rising of many in Israel' (2:34). Whatever she heard and saw, her reaction was immediate: she 'began to praise God and to speak about the child to all who were looking for the redemption of Jerusalem' (2:38).

Anna, then, despite her years, is another woman who enjoys a privileged position. Following the unlikely witnesses to the newborn Messiah in the person of despised shepherds, Anna is an equally improbable evangelist. And it is remarkable that probably the next enthusiastic witness to Jesus, many years later, will again be a woman – not elderly this time, but a foreigner, from Samaria.

Anna and Simeon in their old age are rewarded by God for their faithful waiting, and they both respond with immediate prophetic praise.

Prophets and Poets in the Early Church

The writings of Paul indicate that the gift of prophecy was given to both men and women and there is no indication that women were regarded any less favourably than their male counterparts. No one is singled out, although there is the intriguing detail in Acts 21 that the four daughters of the evangelist Philip each had the gift of prophecy (21:9). It is not unknown for spiritual gifts to pass from one generation of a family to the next, and it may be that in this case a Christian home fostered an atmosphere in which the girls could develop such a gift.

The early church seems to have been no more free of false women prophets than was Judah in the time of Ezekiel. Revelation 2 delivers a stern warning to the church in Thyatira because it tolerates Jezebel 'who calls herself a prophet' (2:20), who encourages idolatry and refuses to repent of her sexual immorality. Such is the cost of equality.

Like prophecy, musical expression in the Bible is not confined to either men or women. Singers and dancers appear at moments of celebration in the Old Testament; the congregation contributed hymns (1 Corinthians 14:26) in the New Testament. And although these references are few and far between, it is perhaps sufficient to note that in celebration and worship women have their distinctive gifts to contribute.

The First Prophet of the Modern Age: Hildegard of Bingen (1098–1179)[1]

> O how magnificent is the compassion of the Saving One,
> Who frees all things by his becoming one with human life.
> Divinity breathes into compassion without the chains of sin,
> And so removes heart-breaking pain from that very garment humanity wears.[2]

If you had to choose one woman to embody all the talents of Old Testament women prophets, the twelfth-century prophet and poet Hildegard of Bingen would be a very strong contender. She was a natural leader, heading up her own community; she was also a theologian and an original thinker, a mystic and a spiritual guide. She challenged the male rulers of her day, both religious and secular, and she was an important prophet, calling for justice towards God's creation and experiencing visions of the Last Days. In recent years Hildegard's music and songs have been revived and recorded, enjoying considerable popular success. She has been described as 'a Renaissance woman several centuries before the Renaissance'.[3]

Hildegard was the tenth of ten children to be born into a family of the upper nobility in the German town of Bernersheim. When she was eight she was taken to the Disibode monastery, a Benedictine foundation which had just opened a women's cloister. There Hildegard grew up and studied. In 1136 she was chosen to lead the community, whereupon she broke away from the monastery, eventually moving into a new cloister near the modern town of Bingen. By then she had completed her first book, *Scivias* ('know the ways') and was attracting many women to live and study with her. *Scivias* (written between 1141 and 1151) is a series of visions depicting the world from Creation and Fall through to the Last Days. Each vision was painted by women illuminators (for Hildegard received her visions pictorially) and is described in words and interpreted by a heavenly voice.

Later in her life Hildegard founded a second convent (today the Abbey of St Hildegard near Rudesheim). Another book written between 1163 and 1173, *The Book of Divine Works*, is a visionary trilogy using many twelfth-century ideas about the end of time. One of the visions begins with a message that could have come from a modern ecologist: 'This is what the Son says to the Father. "In the beginning all created things turned green. In the middle period flowers bloomed, but afterward the greening power of life lessened"' (231). This is the familiar idea of the world being in decay, but Hildegard's vision is of the world's life-giving resources gradually drying up as the end approaches. Again she describes the pictorial form of her visions, although the text itself was not illustrated until after her death. In addition there are powerful letters and sermons, often addressed to some of the most influential people of her time.

Towards the end of her life Hildegard collected together her songs and accompanying music and called them 'The Symphony of the Harmony of Heavenly Revelations'. She also wrote an opera, *Play of the Virtues*, which was the musical setting of a morality play. Like the Old Testament 'singing-women' she celebrated the power of God, but brings in her own vision in which the earth itself has a central role.

Like Catherine of Siena, Hildegard was not afraid to challenge papal authority if she felt it was being misused or indeed underused. In a letter of 1153 to the aging Pope Anastasius IV she attacks him for being weak and allowing himself to be manipulated:

> You are becoming weary, too tired to restrain the arrogant boastfulness of people to whom you have trusted your heart. Why do you not call these shipwrecked people back? They can be rescued from serious danger only through your help. (273)

In more prophetic vein she continues:

> You despise God when you don't hurl from yourself the evil but, even worse, embrace it and kiss it by silently tolerating corrupt men. The whole Earth is in confusion on account of the ever recurring false teaching whereby human beings love what God has brought to nothing. And you, O Rome, are like one in the throes of death. You will be so shaken that the strength of your feet, the

feet on which you now stand, will disappear. For you don't love the King's daughter, justice, with glowing love but as in a delirium of sleep so that you push her away from you. (275)

She concludes:

And so, O man, stand upon the right way and God will rescue you. God will lead you back to the fold of blessing and election and you will live forever. (276)

Hildegard based her writing and teaching on Scripture and she was a gifted commentator on biblical texts. Barbara Newman[4] sums up her mission as being 'to unlock the mysteries of Scripture, to proclaim the way of salvation, to admonish priests and prelates, to instruct the people of God'. Among her letters is one to no less a person than Archbishop Eberhard of Salzburg who had written to her asking for prayer and advice. Hildegard in her reply suggests that he is failing to see his striving for God and his concern for his people as a unity:

After all, Christ too adhered to heavenly things and yet at the same time he drew close to the people. It stands written in Scripture: 'I say, "You are gods, of the Most High, all of you"' (Psalm 82:6). I interpret his text to mean that we are 'gods' in relation to the Divine and 'sons of the Most High' in our concern for the people. (283)

On a more personal note, Hildegard allows her Earth-oriented mysticism to shine through in a letter to Bertha, Queen of Greece and Empress of Byzantium, who longs for a son:

God's Spirit breathes and speaks: in wintertime, God takes care of the branch that is love. In summer, God causes that same branch to be green and to sprout with blossoms. God removes diseased outgrowths that could do harm to the branch. (292)

Hildegard's songs are simple yet distinctive in their message. For example, her short hymn 'De Spiritu Sancto' ('To the Holy Spirit') extols the creating and cleansing power of the Spirit moving on the earth.

Holy Spirit, making life alive,
Moving in all things, root of all created being,
Cleansing the cosmos of every impurity, effacing guilt,
    anointing wounds.
You are lustrous and praiseworthy life,
You waken and re-awaken everything that is. (373)

Her natural imagery pervades all aspects of her spirituality. Her hymn 'De Sancta Maria' ('To Mary') begins:

Hail to you, O greenest, most fertile branch! (379)

And her song to St Disibode, founder of her first spiritual home echoes the theme:

O life-giving greenness of God's hand!
Through you, God has planted an orchard. (391)

Ultimately, though, Hildegard is most conscious of her own humility in the face of divine power, and her weakness in the face of earthly ones. This was not for her an impediment but an affirmation of biblical principles.

While modern music lovers have developed an enthusiasm for Hildegard's music and poetry, in the context of church history it is perhaps her prophetic voice which is the more distinctive. The modern prophet, Rosemary Radford Ruether concludes: 'Hildegard could and did speak ... with a thunderous voice to the greatest men of her day.'[5]

An 'Imperfect Soul': Christina Rossetti (1830–94)

> What can I give him
> Poor as I am
> If I were a shepherd
> I would bring a lamb;
> If I were a wise man
> I would do my part,
> Yet what I can I give him
> Give my heart.

Few people would deny that the Victorian poet Christina Rossetti did indeed give her heart to her Lord, not only through her poetry, which was acclaimed in her own day, but also through extensive charitable work and in the writing of devotional biblical commentaries. Alleged to have been disappointed in love, Christina never married, but gave over much of her life to looking after her beloved mother, who lived until Christina was in her fifties. During much of the last century Christina's popularity waned, and her poems were generally deemed too 'sentimental' for modern tastes. More recently though there has been renewed interest in her poetry and in her close association with the pre-Raphaelites through her artist brother Dante Gabriel Rossetti.

Born into a family which, although resident in London, was more Italian than English, Christina often felt she was overshadowed by her talented sister and brothers. Her own talent, though, emerged at an early age and her first known poem is a birthday tribute to her mother, written when she was eleven. One of her biographers notes, 'Though not a poem to shake the world, it has a grace and poise unlike the first attempts of most young poets. Christina, listening at the fireside to her father's poems and her mother's Bible reading, had absorbed more than anyone realised.'[6] As this picture suggests, religion was important to the young Christina. For much of her life she was a faithful member of Christ Church in Albany Street, whose vicar became a leading light in the Oxford Movement. Years later Christina was to write enthusiastically about a rather dubious sounding addition to the church's decoration, 'a large red cross reared high in the Chancel arch'.[7] Anglo-Catholicism evidently appealed to Christina, although for much of her life she struggled to understand how she might be numbered among the elect.

The poems Christina wrote as a young woman reveal the acute observation of the natural world which came to characterize all her work, intermingled with religious sentiment. A frequent theme is the tension between divine and earthly love, as Christina struggled against what she saw as a sinful love of the world. It was a time of broken engagements: one poem speaks of a lovers' parting ordained by God and includes the lines:

> God's Love is higher than mine,
> Christ's tenfold proved,
> Yet even I would die
> For thee Beloved.[8]

There was also disappointment that her poems were not being as well received as she thought they should be. In 1868 she complained of the 'poetical barrenness that has crept over me this long while past'.[9] By the 1870s, though, she seemed to have become resigned to her lot, and the last years of her life were given over to religious poems and commentaries, as she took an increasing stand against what she saw as the growing secularization of the time. A letter written in 1872 expresses her characteristic delight at a stay in the Sussex countryside: 'a most charming place with greenness and flowers to refresh our London eyes, and a small population of beasts and birds around us'.[10]

The optimistic side of Christina's faith for others is shown in several letters to her friend Amelia Heimann after the death of Amelia's husband:

I nourish a hope that the brightness of a future common joy awaits us, after all, in the next world. Past, present, future; all are solemn to middleaged eyes; and you and I have attained middle age together. Pardon me my solemn words: for why should old friends never dive below the surface, and look through time into eternity?[11]

A few months later, shortly before the death of her sister Maria, she wrote to another friend:

Happily in proportion as earthly hope dies out heavenly hope glows and kindles, so evident is the Grace of God in our dear Maria's patience and loving conformity to the Divine Will.[12]

Christina espoused various causes during her lifetime. In the late 1870s she considered the question of women's suffrage, and although she felt that married women should have the vote and that female MPs might be a good thing, she could not escape what she saw as the 'unalterable distinction' between men and women in the Bible. Her conviction remained that women's greatness lay in their 'mighty maternal love'.[13] Around the same time she also took up the issue of animal vivisection, and wrote in aid of the funds of the anti-vivisectionists a truly dreadful poem beginning:

> Pity the sorrows of a poor old Dog
> Who wags his tail a-begging in his need.[14]

In middle age Christina achieved the success she had longed for, while becoming increasingly secluded and given over to devotional matters. A letter of 1885 sums up her view of her art: 'Just because poetry *is* a gift . . . I am not surprised to find myself unable to summon it at will and use it according to my own choice.'[15]

So we may perhaps see in Christina, though not one of the poetic greats, more than a trace of those unnamed biblical women who also used their gift in celebration of God and of his greatness in the created world. Frances Thomas's judgement of her is an 'imperfect soul striving towards a clarity of faith and love that it can never quite attain'.[16] Perhaps a more memorable appraisal, though, is that of Arthur Symms: 'We read her as though we are eavesdropping on the dialogue of a soul with God.'[17]

A Prophet for Our Time: Rosemary Radford Ruether

If it is difficult to slot people of the past into discrete categories, it is virtually impossible to do this with a woman who is currently at the height of her powers, exercising formidable talents as a prolific writer, teacher, speaker and academic. Yet it is as a prophet that the American Rosemary Radford Ruether may in the end best be acclaimed, and she has readily been acknowledged as such, one writer ranking her alongside Martin Luther King Jr and the Peruvian theologian Gustavo Gutierrez.[18]

Ruether was born of a Roman Catholic mother and Episcopalian father, and initially she majored in Classics.

She describes herself as being 'disposed ... to see both positive and negative aspects of the Jewish and Christian traditions and the ancient pagan traditions, and to be sceptical of exclusivistic views on either side',[19] an attitude which seems to characterize her entire work.

Ruether's theological thinking seems to have been moulded by two separate movements. The first was 1960s feminism in the United States, where the leading writers were either ignoring religion, as was the case, for example, with Betty Friedan, or else examining it in the light of their own theories only to reject it – the standpoint of Mary Daly. Ruether's answer to this, in line with the response of at least parts of the church, was to argue that religion could, on the contrary, be instrumental in the struggle for women's rights. Although remaining a Roman Catholic, Ruether adopted a broadly ecumenical Christianity, while fostering a concern for environmentalism and cultural tradition.

In this she was slightly in advance of the other formative influence in her life, liberation theology. This was of course developed primarily in South America in the 1970s and 1980s, as a consequence of the encouragement of lay participation provided by Vatican II and in response to the oppressive dictatorships which were causing hardship and suffering in countries across the continent. Like these new theologians Ruether expressed what William Ramsay terms a 'loving criticism of her church's hierarchical system'.[20] He continues, '[A]s a Christian she opposes the domination, which sometimes becomes almost enslavement, of any people by others.'[21] This is at the heart of Ruether's concerns as she examines what she sees as the oldest form of human oppression, sexism, throughout Judaeo-Christian history. In a letter to Thomas Merton in 1967, Ruether expressed her concerns about the church itself:

It was not founded by Christ, but by history ... The Church as historical vehicle carries the words about this good news, but in its own substance exhibits more deeply than anywhere else this fallenness and estrangement which is the condition from which God is saving his creation.[22]

Ruether's insightful approach to the Bible lends a particularly attractive flavour to her writing. Rather than simply dismiss the Old Testament writings as unacceptably sexist, she recognizes that sexist passages simply reflect the culture in which they were written. Her view of the prophets is a positive one, as she sees them as 'the central tradition by which Biblical faith constantly criticizes and renews itself and its own vision'.[23] In that the prophets spoke out against oppression she sees them as the precursors of feminist theology, arguing for justice for women. From the Gospels Ruether recognizes Jesus' concern and respect for women, and his example in placing men and women on an equal footing. She concludes: 'The New Testament and Patristic message of the inclusion of women in the image of God redeemed in Christ ... activated women as seeking and acting on this offer of redemption.'[24]

Although hugely critical of the dismissive attitude to women on the part of early and Scholastic theologians, quoting as an example Aquinas' view of women as 'misbegotten males', Ruether rejoices in the fact that although women were not allowed to teach publicly, their writings were preserved in religious institutions, and she welcomes the inclusion of women as prophets in the medieval church: 'As direct vehicles of God's presence and voice, women both denounced evils and pointed to the way of restored life with God',[25] a description that could equally well be applied to Ruether herself. She cannot refrain from adding, though, that women's revelatory experiences still had to be validated by the men who held ecclesiastical power and authority.

Ruether had already developed her thesis in a substantial historical work co-written with Rosemary Skinner Keller.[26] In it the authors examine the religious role of women, first in the course of the nineteenth century and in revivalist movements, and they highlight the active preaching ministry of many women and their egalitarian thought. The twentieth century, though, they see as marked by conflicting trends: the charismatic tradition as it appears largely outside the church, which is 'inclusive of women precisely because it validated the presence of the Spirit',[27] as against a reactionary view of women in the 1930s and a new subordination of women which persisted until an evangelical feminism emerged in the 1960s. This account does much to illuminate the role of women in religious history and deserves to be regarded as a key contribution to the subject.

In *Women and Redemption* Ruether summarizes her theology like this: 'God is not a "being" removed from creation, ruling it from outside in the manner of a patriarchal ruler; God is the source of being that underlies creation and grounds its nature and future potential for continual transformative renewal in *biophilic maturity*', a learned phrase by which she means 'human nature being rooted in God'.[28] She has, however, disarmingly expressed unease about the academic discipline of theology: 'I distrust all academic theology. Only theology bred in the crucible of experience is any good.'[29]

Like liberation theologians who approach biblical texts from the standpoint of the poor and oppressed, Ruether includes within her theology a view 'from the bottom' or 'from the underside' which she puts together with a view 'from the other end', a vision of the transformation of creation. Again hers is a balanced approach as she couples this with a warning that victims themselves are 'not infallible nor without their own delusions and potential to misuse power'.[30] Similarly, her view of men preserves the gospel example of equality. She warns against 'reverse racism' whereby women may affirm themselves in such a way as to diminish male humanity, arguing that anything in religion or society that diminishes one group as less than fully human diminishes everyone. Her view of men's attitude to feminism is a perceptive one, proposing that men either reject the idea that women are in any way oppressed and trivialize their views, or they recognize sexism as an issue, see that they too may be the victims of it, and become almost more feminist than the feminists.

A leading historian of liberation theology recognizes in Ruether 'one of the most prolific and creative theologians on the contemporary scene' and 'an outstanding feminist liberation theologian and leader'.[31] Among feminists she is surely outstanding for her balanced objectivity and depth of intellectual inquiry. Like the women prophets of the Old Testament Ruether is also gifted in speaking out with a clear and confident voice, and with them too one senses in her a sure faith in a just and liberating God.

8

Women Together

Where you go, I will go; where you lodge, I will lodge.
(Ruth 1:16)

Loving Across Cultures: Ruth and Naomi (The Book of Ruth)

Most critics of the Book of Ruth make the point that this lovely short story has something of a timeless quality. Despite the inclusion of some details of Deuteronomic and Levitical law, there is little to limit it to any particular time or indeed place. On the other hand, the closing verses do give it a special place in the history of Israel. Ruth's son Obed, born in Bethlehem, was to be the grandfather of David – and therefore the ancestor of Jesus Christ (cf. Matthew 1:5) – and this story may have had the purpose of explaining how David's great-grandmother came to be a Moabite.

Central to the story is the difference in nationality between Ruth and Naomi, the young woman and her mother-in-law, whose deep affection and respect for each other sets them apart from other women in the Bible. Both suffer great loss: Ruth is bereaved of her husband, Naomi's son, while Naomi also loses her second son about the same time, having been widowed some ten years earlier. They are alone apart from each other and the other daughter-in-law, Orpah, who is persuaded to return home to her own family and the chance of a second marriage.

Not only does Ruth 'cling' to her mother-in-law. She willingly renounces her own people to be with her: 'your people shall be my people, and your God my God' (Ruth 1:16), which puts an end to Naomi's attempts to send Ruth home. They arrive in Judah at harvest time, a time of richness and plenty which marks the beginning of the change in their fortunes from the emptiness which they feel both on account of their bereavements and because of the lack of food they had suffered in Moab, to a time of emotional and physical fullness and satisfaction.

Together the two women work to improve their lot. Ruth goes willingly into the harvest fields to provide for them both, while Naomi reflects on how she may find a home for her daughter-in-law: 'My daughter, I need to seek some security for you, that it may be well with you' (3:1). And it is notable that Boaz, the farmer who will bring their story to a happy and successful conclusion, is as inclined to natural kindness and upright behaviour as the two women themselves. Boaz acts initially as Ruth's protector because he admires her devotion to Naomi, and Ruth is grateful for his kindness to a foreigner: 'May I continue to find favour in your sight, my Lord, for you have comforted me and spoken kindly to your servant, though I am not one of your servants' (2:13).

Ruth's complete trust in her mother-in-law is demonstrated in her willingness to go along with Naomi's plan, which has her going to Boaz at midnight and 'lying at his feet'. In this compromising situation Boaz once again acknowledges Ruth's qualities: 'This last instance of your loyalty is better than the first; you have not gone after young men, whether poor or rich' (3:10) and he plans their future.

The outcome of the story depends on an unexpected move by Naomi who puts part of her husband's land up for sale (this has not previously been mentioned as an option, in spite of the women's apparent destitution when they arrived in Bethlehem). There are also some legal complications: Naomi's next of kin, who is not Boaz although he is next in line after that, was by custom expected to buy the land to keep it in the family. In addition it is suggested that Ruth (who otherwise would have married her husband's brother, had he survived) should marry the purchaser, whereupon the unnamed next of kin opts out of the deal, on the grounds that this would adversely affect his own chain of inheritance. (Any children of a marriage to Ruth would have caused unspecified legal problems, although the kinsman, it seems, would have accepted Naomi who was past child-bearing age.) These legal complications, however, seem less important than the overall message: that Naomi is enabling her daughter-in-law's future to be secure.

As Boaz's marriage to Ruth moves to a rapid conclusion, the local elders show that they too have fully accepted the foreigner and are willing to make her part of their national history: 'May the Lord make the woman who is coming into your house like Rachel and Leah, who together built up the house of Israel ... and, through the children that the Lord will give you by this young woman, may your house be like the house of Perez, whom Tamah bore to Judah' (4:11, 12).

Marriage does nothing to shake the bond between Ruth and Naomi. On the contrary, it provides the opportunity for Naomi to find fulfilment and her own happy ending. Local people offer a comment on the relationship between the two women as they bring Ruth's baby son Obed to Naomi for her to care for as her own: 'Your daughter-in-law who loves you, who is more to you than seven sons, has borne him' (4.15). So Ruth is safely settled with a second husband of exemplary character, while Naomi brings up the child, the future grandfather of David the King, which has the effect of associating her too with the royal line. But the detail of the baby, although important for biblical history, far from overshadowing the relationship between two women which is the central feature of the whole story, simply enhances it.

Although God plays no obvious part in the story of Ruth and Naomi, it is very clear that their love for each other wins divine approval. It could be that the character of God himself is the model for their behaviour. In 1:8, the line 'May the Lord deal kindly with you' translates the Hebrew noun *hesed*, a characteristic of God which generally appears in English as 'loving kindness', and it is this above all which also characterizes the two women's feelings for each other.

God's guidance, though not explicit, may be detected in bringing about the first meeting between Ruth and her near kinsman Boaz: 'As it happened, she came to the part of the field belonging to Boaz, who was of the family of Elimelech' (2:3). And in praising Ruth's care for Naomi, Boaz recognizes a relationship which is pleasing to God: 'May the Lord reward you for your deeds, and may you have a full reward from the Lord, the God of Israel, under whose wings you have come for refuge!' (2:12). In turn Naomi acknowledges the presence of God and his 'loving kindness' at work through Boaz: 'Blessed be he by the Lord, whose kindness has not forsaken the living or the dead!' (2:20). In every respect, it seems, Boaz is a worthy addition to the women's family, though at no point in the story is it stated that Boaz and Naomi actually meet. Finally, Naomi herself is blessed by God. As the local women put it, '[The Lord] shall be to you a restorer of life and a nourisher of your old age' (4:15).

There are a number of themes running through the Book of Ruth, among them that of the preservation of the family line, as well as, according to some commentators, a comment on the post-exilic restrictions on mixed marriages set out in Ezra 9–10 and Nehemiah 13:23–9.[1] Yet it is always the relationship between the two women that stands out, characterized above all by their love and kindness. Katrina Larkin concludes: 'It is the view of the rabbis that the purpose of Ruth is "to teach how great is the reward of those who do deeds of kindness" (*Ruth R.* 2.13) ... and perhaps the rabbis have correctly identified the one function of Ruth that most clearly transcends its original setting.'[2]

Beloved Disciples: Mary and Martha (Luke 10:38–42; John 11:1–44; 12:1–8)

The household of Mary, Martha and Lazarus in Bethany is the setting for a rare picture in the Gospels: Jesus among friends he loved and who loved him. He relaxed at their home and wept with them in their distress. The two sisters were also privileged to witness the greatest moment in Jesus' ministry before he went to the cross, when he restored life to their dead brother.

Yet the most familiar view of Mary and Martha is typically a distorted one. A single incident reported only by Luke (10:38–42) shows Martha apparently complaining at the demands of her role as a hostess – she was 'distracted by her many tasks' (10:40) – while her sister sat around listening to Jesus. So Martha gets characterized as the often unacceptably busy one, preoccupied with domestic duties, while Mary is praised for taking time to listen for the short period that Jesus is among them. Medieval theologians used the story as their justification for attributing greater importance to a life of contemplation than to a life of service.

This is surely a distortion, and such a marked difference

in character is not to be found in John's Gospel. Martha's role is an essential one: to offer hospitality and to serve her special guest. It is not that she begrudges this service; rather that, like most of us in a similar situation, she gets irritated by her sister's inactivity. Jesus' reaction is a gentle defence of Mary rather than an outright criticism of Martha's way of serving him. When it comes to Christian service the two things are complementary: listening to the Lord in quiet and offering him active service. Neither is wrong: both are to be desired. The two sisters, through their natural inclinations, symbolize this to perfection.

A careful reading of John 11, on the other hand, tends to give Martha the dominant role. She comes across as a woman of faith and understanding, and her statement of belief in Jesus shows greater perception and maturity than anything we hear from the male disciples.

Perhaps in keeping with Martha's preference for activity, it is she who goes out to meet Jesus when news reaches them of his imminent arrival. (It is worth remembering that Jesus' love for this family is such that he undertakes the journey back to Judea against the advice of his disciples who warn him of the personal danger he faces there.)

Martha's faith is evident when she greets Jesus: 'Lord if you had been here my brother would not have died. But even now I know that God will give you whatever you ask of him' (John 11:21-2). Her understanding of resurrection is what C. K. Barrett terms that of 'orthodox Pharisaism'[3] and this belief that the dead will rise to life on the last day will become that of the early church. The important thing about Martha's statement, though, is that it gives Jesus the opportunity to make the greatest of all his 'I am' declarations: 'I am the resurrection and the life.' And in one sense we might see Martha as the believing counterpart to the questioning Thomas, who similarly in John's Gospel provides Jesus with the questions which provoke some of his most profound sayings. Martha's response to Jesus' reply is one of great maturity, comparable to Thomas' exclamation in 20:28, 'My Lord and my God'. She says, 'Yes, Lord, I believe that you are the Messiah, the Son of God, the one who is coming into the world' (11:27), affirming her belief with the use of no fewer than three messianic titles.

Martha's depth of perception is shown again when she fetches Mary. She does it 'privately', perhaps sensing that the large crowd who would follow Jesus once they saw what was going on would have little understanding of his actions. This caution is more than justified by the subsequent reaction of the Jews: some believed but others went off to the Pharisees to report Jesus' latest 'sign', which simply hardens their resolve to kill him.

After his conversation with Martha, Jesus turns to Mary. There is little doubt that Mary shares her sister's faith in him, and she echoes Martha's words, 'Lord if you had been here my brother would not have died' (11:32, cf. 11:21). But she goes no further than that, perhaps suggesting that she does not share the same degree of insight as Martha into their friend's true nature. What is striking about this conversation, though, is her grief which is also shared by Jesus. John Marsh comments, 'As a picture of a disciple in sorrow and loss going out to meet her Lord [Mary] is a universal symbol of the distressed disciple',[4] and one might also reflect that this is a unique image in the New Testament.

The scene at Lazarus' tomb indicates that despite her insights, Martha still stops short of being able to see the faith of her understanding translated into reality. She protests that her brother's corpse will already be too decayed for Jesus to do anything. Again Jesus responds by allowing her a further glimpse of his true nature: 'Did I not tell you

that if you believed you would see the glory of God?'
(11:40).

The raising of Lazarus is, then, the opportunity for the
evangelist to present a detailed portrayal of two women
disciples whose faith sets them apart from the others, and
whose home is a welcome place of refuge for their Lord.
There is also in John's Gospel an extra twist to their story.
At the beginning of chapter 12, John attributes the anointing of Jesus not to an anonymous sinner but to Mary of
Bethany, so giving the action added significance. Once
again Martha is the hostess, serving at table. Mary offers
a different form of service, breaking open expensive oint-
ment over Jesus' feet and drying them with her hair. She
does not perform the action of anointing a king: that would
mean anointing his head. Marsh suggests that this shows
her understanding that Jesus is not yet king – that will
come only with his death – and that his gift of resurrection
to new life for those who believe is associated with the
forgiveness of sins. If this is so, then we have at the end
of this story of two sisters an image of them equal in the
depth of their faith. And despite their natural differences
in character, they are united in their love and service and
deep friendship for Jesus their Lord.

A Community in Shetland: Sister Agnes

In 1984, an Anglican Franciscan nun left the security of a
community in Devon, which had been her home for the
past twenty years, to live a solitary life on Fetlar. This is
a small island off the coast of the main island of Shetland. It
is a beautiful and remote place, though lashed by punishing
winds and blizzards during the long harsh winters. It was
here that Sister Agnes came in response to God's call to
bring the religious life to the Scottish islands, long steeped
in Celtic tradition.

Sister Agnes was not quite alone. Apart from a small local community there was her old friend Rosemary who, though not a Sister herself, had come to live nearby and lived as an associate with Sister Agnes, sharing the Divine Offices with her and working alongside her. Even so, Sister Agnes was essentially a community of one and she rejoiced in her solitude. Yet at the back of her mind was the knowledge that God had given her a further call – to live not as a solitary but to establish a community. But the longer she remained alone, the more remote that call seemed to be. She wrote:

> No one, least of all myself, could say that I was the type to found an Order and anyway, I had grown very used to being on my own. Could I, now, enjoy sharing all this space and freedom, the glory of this place and a life lived for God? Could I cope, in fact, with living so closely alongside another human being?
>
> Maybe I was meant to go on and develop the solitary vocation instead? Now that was a thought that appealed to me![5]

In 1988 Sister Agnes had written a book describing her initial call to Fetlar, in which she wrote: 'Why was I so magnetised to the Isles? . . . I was magnetised because God was calling me to them.'[6] She followed this up in 1994 with a sequel, *The Song of the Lark*, an honest view of her inner struggles as she gradually moved from being a solitary nun to being part of a growing community. In her careful, sometimes poetic, account, Sister Agnes allows the reader to imagine this profound change by setting passages from the present alongside her narrative of the past. So almost as soon as she has set down her initial doubts she continues: 'I, who sought solitude, have founded an Order.

I, who sought the embrace of God, am now able to embrace others and, with them, to be enfolded by Him.'[7] And her description of how she moved from one state to the other must strike a chord with any women who have faced the not inconsiderable challenge of living and working together.

The main hurdle which Sister Agnes had to overcome was the arrival of Mary – a widowed lady with a strong call herself – to live with Sister Agnes on Fetlar. The two women could hardly have been more different in character:

> Mary is impulsive as well as dynamic, and often disorganised, which in contrast to my own over-tidy, sometimes pernickety, nature has caused many a friction.[8]

There was a difference in spiritual inclination: Sister Agnes followed an Anglo-Catholic tradition, Mary was an evangelical. Mary was naturally demonstrative, while Sister Agnes at first shrank from physical contact, describing how on one occasion Mary hugged her 'and involuntarily, not meaning to, I stiffened', whereupon Mary told her, 'I'd like you to know that, in spite of your twenty-plus years in a convent, for me, touch is very important.' Sister Mary found herself speechless and feeling intensely vulnerable. That was to change, with Sister Agnes later describing, without comment, how she and Mary 'flung their arms around each other in a final embrace' in one of their more recent moments of parting.[9]

Mary had paid a number of visits to Fetlar at different times of the year before Sister Agnes was persuaded that together they should form the heart of a new community. The turning point seemed to come when Mary drew attention to the Old Testament story of Ruth and Naomi: '"I want to share with you what my Bible reading was today . . . It was about Ruth and Naomi . . . about real trust and real friendship from Ruth 1.14 and 16. Would you read it too, and share my joy?" Something inside me snapped, long overdue and long needed.'[10] So Sister Agnes drew up a plan for her new Order – the Society of Our Lady of the Isles (SOLI) – which is possibly the newest Order in the Anglican Communion. It was to be constructed like a wheel with God at the centre surrounded by a small inner circle of Sisters in vows, whose calling is to be home-based, living out the gospel in prayer and hospitality. Radiating out from there are the spokes – the Oblate Sisters – who work in the community. They in turn are surrounded by a still wider circle of friends who live nearby and share in the Sisters' daily life and work. The final outer circle is known as the Caim – women and men who support the community prayerfully and financially and with a simple lifestyle, while living and working away from it. Although potentially a very big wheel, the innermost circle still remains tiny at the point where Sister Agnes ends her story.

Five years after Sister Agnes left her Devon community, Mary was admitted to the Society of Our Lady of the Isles, taking the name Sister Mary Clare, and at the same ceremony Sister Agnes was honoured as the new community's foundress. So began a new chapter in her life, but by this time she was already referring to the group which was gathering round her as 'our family', and Mary soon became 'my dear Sister'. Other possible members of the community were also beginning to come on the scene. There was the New Zealander Pat, a teacher, who, to test her calling to a more isolated existence, took a job in a school in a remote rural area. When she eventually visited Fetlar the Sisters, loving her combination of humour and commonsense, 'felt strongly that God was asking her to come . . . and join forces with us as a member of the community'.[11]

Then there was Rose, who eventually came to live on

Fetlar but as the island nurse rather than as a member of the Order. Of her, Sister Agnes writes, 'Perhaps [the Lord] has tried, tested and lifted her down again and is waiting patiently until the right cavity for her exact and unique shape will appear.'[12] Yet there are others waiting in the wings, whom the one-time solitary nun who is now in her sixties and still enjoying a very basic lifestyle, looks forward to receiving with great hope: 'There are a number of women waiting and hoping at the end of a period of time to join us. Are we then . . . I pray so . . . being built up as living stones into a spiritual house?'[13] It is hard to imagine the Sister who so loved the solitary life making such a comment but now she is truly committed to being among women together.

The Lowest of the Low: The Christian Dalit Women of India

In the twenty-first century, communities of women living together are becoming increasingly hard to find, with few younger women feeling a call to this kind of religious life. Much more common, though, are groupings of women, particularly in developing countries, who have been brought together by a shared longing for social, political and religious freedom and a determination to achieve it. Although often geographically distant from each other, these groups together speak with a voice that demands to be heard. These women together are, in a sense, the successors to communities of holy women of the past, and perhaps too to the early suffragettes. They form what are arguably the most significant women's movements in today's world, and they are bound together in a common cause and with a mutual respect which echoes the ancient relationships of biblical women.

In the 1980s and 1990s, women's voices came to be

heard in Christian communities in South America and else-where where liberation theology was offering them new insights into the Bible. They found inspiration in the experi-ences of women in both the Old and New Testaments which demonstrated in particular God's liberating love for women of all times. Gifted exponents of biblical texts and some outstanding leaders have emerged, among them Aruna Gnanadason, the Indian theologian, and Mercy Amba Oduyoye from Ghana.

The Christian *dalit* movement in India provides a not-able contemporary example of women's religious con-sciousness combining with an urgent desire for social reform. The *dalit* movement itself began in the 1980s as a general liberation of the poor and oppressed in India and a fight against caste discrimination. The caste system is ancient, dating back to at least the second century BC. It is built on a hierarchy of four orders, from the priestly caste down through the warrior caste, to the traders and artisans, and, finally, manual workers, who are divided into 'touchables' and 'untouchables'. The 'untouchables' are the people who do the lowest manual tasks, such as sweeping and scavenging, and these are the *dalits* (the word means 'oppressed' or 'downtrodden'). It is estimated that today fifteen million of the twenty million Christians in India fall into this category. The large numbers are attrib-uted to the *dalits*' desire to escape from Hindu culture, in the hope of improving their status in a new religion, and there are also many *dalits* in the Islamic, Sikh and Buddhist religions for the same reason. Yet discrimination has fol-lowed the *dalits* into the church, where they are still often required to sit in specially designated places and to bury their dead in separate burial grounds.[14]

Women are often referred to as the '*dalit* among *dalits* and the downtrodden among the downtrodden', suffering sexual discrimination over and above that of caste, and

accounts of the inhuman and dangerous conditions in
which many of them live make depressing reading. Yet out
of all this Christian women are beginning to be heard, and
indeed read. One South Indian woman has written a poem
called 'Dalit Women Society's Firewood' which ends like
this:

> We are not prostitutes,
> We are toilers with self-respect,
> We are dalit women proud,
> We are the providers for humanity,
>
> Did God ordain our fate?
> Will men decide our lives?
> Are we faggots for burning in the funeral pyre?
> No, we will rise and free ourselves.[15]

Swarnalatha Devi has movingly described the solidarity
of a group of some four hundred Christian *dalit* women
in the state of Andhra Pradesh as with their men they
boarded a train for Madras, each laden with bags and
children:

> They prayed before they boarded the train, as a group,
> as a community. They were migrating to other places
> for agricultural work ... In the new places they have
> to live under trees or in open places or sometimes in the
> cattle sheds. During this period they virtually live under
> the pleasure and the will of the landlords and middle-
> men. They will continue to pray and sing and struggle.
>
> They are the ones who are the givers to the Church.
> They are the ones who are the cross-bearers of the
>   congregation.
> They are the ones who are the torch-bearers of the faith.[16]

She goes on to cite the case of another, smaller group whose sons, husbands and brothers had been murdered by brutal landlords, and who started to lead a protest movement from a church compound. They refused to go back to their village, saying:

> We will not go back to our homes stained by our blood and teardrops. We have been buried alive, and we will continue to shout from our living tombs. We will go everywhere, and speak to anyone and do everything to help our *dalits*. We have nothing more to fear.[17]

At every stage of their struggle these women prayed to God and they continue to struggle, firm in their faith that he will liberate them. And Devi's two examples bear witness to the strength of the faith of the *dalit* women and their determination to end the injustice that has beset them for so long.

It should not be concluded from this that *dalit* women are alone in their struggle. Most *dalit* men recognize that women are the most oppressed, although, according to Ruth Manorama, they tend to see the women as 'victims rather than victors'.[18] And things are beginning to change, albeit slowly and unevenly across India. In 1992 the Dalit Solidarity Programme was launched, which brought *dalits* from different areas and religions together to discuss their problems. At their national convention the World Council of Churches (WCC) issued a statement which included the words:

> The WCC is deeply impressed and challenged by the prominent role and leadership of Dalit women in this struggle. The brave and constructive witness of Dalit women is, and will continue to be, a learning experience for the life and mission of the WCC.[19]

Whenever, in the future, the injustices of the caste system are finally brought to an end, women together will surely be seen to be one of the most powerful and effective forces for change, and worthy successors to the biblical women who together contributed much to the histories of Judaism and of Christianity.

Less than Excellent?

Like many modern biographers, biblical writers are often concerned to show their characters in the best possible light. Few among those already discussed can have been totally without flaws, if only we knew about them. But, interestingly, there are in the Bible some women whose character and behaviour makes them thoroughly unlikely candidates for promoting God's purposes. They are recognizably less than excellent, and all the more real to us because of it.

Sarah: 'You cannot be serious' (Genesis 17:15–18:15)

We have already seen Abraham's wife Sarah in a pretty poor light (Chapter 5), first when she 'dealt harshly' with her pregnant maid Hagar (Genesis 16:6), causing her to flee into the desert, and later having Hagar and her son banished (Genesis 21:10). It might be, of course, that on both occasions there were mitigating circumstances. On the first, Sarah was definitely provoked by Hagar, while on the second, she might just have had a theological point, that Isaac and not Ishmael was the heir to God's promise. And I have already pointed out that Abraham willingly went along with it all. But even so, Sarah's harshness, not to say cruelty, strikes a jarring note in someone whom the New Testament will celebrate as a woman of faith (Hebrews 11:11).

In spite of her standing in Old Testament history, it can

hardly be said, on the evidence we have, that Sarah had a particularly happy or risk-free life. The first thing we hear about her is that she was barren (Genesis 11:30), with all that this entailed in her culture in the way of shame and loss of status. The next time we meet her in Genesis is when she and her husband are travelling to Egypt to escape famine. In order to keep Abraham safe Sarah has to pretend to be his sister, in spite of the risk she runs in Pharaoh's household as a result (Genesis 12:10–20). Incredibly, the same demand is made of her in Gerar (Genesis 20) when she is taken by Abimelech. On both occasions the editor seems to assume that Sarah is much younger, an indication that perhaps there is an underlying older story belonging to a different point in the patriarch's life.

When God gives Abraham and Sarah a child in their old age it is of course Sarah who has to add the discomfort of pregnancy and the pain and risk of childbirth to the inevitable aches and pains of growing old. Then, apart from the expulsion of Hagar, we hear nothing more of Sarah until her death (Genesis 23). This has to be one of the great silences of history. Whatever must Sarah have felt when Abraham returned from having almost sacrificed Isaac on a woodpile (Genesis 22)? What did Isaac say to her and she to him – and to her husband? Did she wonder, despite God's repeated promise and blessing, whatever would be asked of her next?

The role of Sarah in the fulfilment of God's promise to Abraham and therefore in the whole future of Israel, is necessarily central. But, as we have seen, Sarah is no paragon of virtue. And the greatest lapse on the part of both Sarah and her husband has to be when they laugh at God.

God's promise to Abraham of a son (Genesis 17:15) is a solemn moment, and it is important because the barren Sarah is explicitly named as the 'mother of nations' (17:17). It may be that Abraham's inappropriate reaction, as he falls on his face in a parody of worship and laughs, presumably with his face concealed, is hidden to ordinary mortals at least. He also voices his doubts inwardly, before suggesting that God might be satisfied with the son of Hagar instead, a suggestion which leads to God's clear promise of the birth of Isaac in the fairly near future. Even so, in the presence of an all-knowing God, Abraham's behaviour falls barely short of blasphemy.

By contrast, Sarah's response to the same news on another occasion is more circumspect, even though she has no reason at first to suppose that it is God's voice that she hears. Unable to take part in Abraham's conversation with the angels whom he unknowingly entertains, Sarah listens at the door and overhears the news that concerns her more than anyone: 'Your wife Sarah will have a son' (Genesis 18:10). Like Abraham, Sarah laughs 'to herself', yet God hears her and questions her behaviour. What follows is unique in Scripture: 'Why did Sarah laugh?' 'I did not laugh', 'Oh yes, you did laugh' (18:13,15).

In human terms Sarah's laughter is fully understandable. Although we may not now reckon her age in quite the same terms as the Genesis editor, it is still made quite clear that for Sarah child-bearing is no longer an option, unless, of course, God intervenes. Not for Sarah the unquestioning joyful and reverent response of Hannah to the end of her barrenness or the faithful submission of Mary. Sarah – at times a cruel woman, but also at times one seriously misused by her husband – responds as if to an earthly joker: 'You cannot be serious.'

Tamar and Rahab

Judas [Judah] begat Phares and Sara of Thamar ... And Salmon begat Booz of Rachab. (Matthew 1:3, 5, Authorized Version)

The early verses of Matthew's Gospel in the unmistakable tones of the King James Bible are not just remarkable for the trouble they cause all but the most skilled lesson readers. In this male-dominated line of descent, from Abraham through David to Jesus, only a handful of women get a mention. Interestingly four of the five come from outside Judah (the exception being Mary herself), and, if we count Ruth's loneliness and vulnerability, these four, in the words of Park Kyung-mi, all have 'an ugly aspect' in their lives,[1] with two of them – Tamar and Rahab – being designated harlots. This extraordinary twist in the great story of human salvation, is echoed at its culmination with Joseph, 'the husband of Mary', who is not of course the father of her child. John Fenton suggests that 'the presence of their names in the genealogy may be in order to draw attention to the strange ways in which divine providence works'.[2]

Matthew's source lies back in 1 Chronicles, with its genealogies of the descendants of Judah in chapters 2 to 4. In 1 Chronicles 2:11, we read that Salma (Salmon) was the father of Boaz, but the Gospel writer has chosen to add in the detail that Rahab was his mother. Tamar, Judah's daughter-in-law, though, is already there.

Tamar: A Family Misbehaves (Genesis 38)

Judah, one of the sons of Jacob, and a leader among them, appears to have moved away from his brothers to settle in Canaanite territory, where he married Bathshua, a Canaanite woman, by whom he had three sons. He then chose a Canaanite wife for the eldest, who died without issue ('the Lord put him to death' Genesis 38:7). Following the custom of the time, Judah passed this wife Tamar to the next son, who also displeased God and came to a similar end. Perhaps fearful that Tamar was in some way responsible for the family's misfortunes, Judah sent Tamar home to her father and did not give her to the remaining, youngest, son as tradition would have required.

The custom that lies behind the subsequent union of Judah himself and his twice-married daughter-in-law Tamar is obscure. According to Gerhard von Rad, married women might give themselves to strangers on the strength of an oath made to the pagan goddess of love, Astarte. So the newly widowed Judah finds Tamar on the roadside, no longer dressed as a widow, but offering herself to him as a passer-by. Judah readily agrees to her demands for pledges, even though these will in due course identify him.

The consequences are almost inevitable: 'About three months later Judah was told, "Your daughter-in-law Tamar has played the whore; moreover she is pregnant as a result of whoredom"' (Genesis 38:24). Sentenced to death, Tamar reveals the identity of her lover. From this point onwards she is seen as the more 'righteous' of the two. Judah recognizes that he was at fault in not giving her to his remaining son, thereby depriving her of her status and security, and does not make any further claims on her himself.

Despite Tamar's dubious behaviour – brought about by Judah's unjust treatment of her – she is blessed. She gives birth to twin boys – Perez and Zerah – who will create new family lines. The account in Numbers 26 of a census ordered by Moses and Aaron tells us that along with the Shelanites (descended from Judah and Bathshua's third son) their descendants numbered 76,500 – a significant proportion of the overall total of Israelites which exceeded 600,000. For the sake of this outcome, comments von Rad, Tamar 'drags herself and Judah into serious guilt'.[3] Out of the unpromising situation in which both Judah and Tamar do wrong, God's promise of descendants, originally given to Abraham, is honoured.

Rahab: Life-saving Lies (Joshua 2)

Tamar takes extreme measures in order to secure her own future, and, almost incidentally, furthers God's purposes for his chosen people. Her 'whoredom' is a one-off incident, which not only achieves the result she wanted but also enables God's promise to be honoured further.

Rahab, on the other hand, is a prostitute by profession. She comes into the story of God's promise – this time the promise of land rather than descendants – because her Jericho home was in a particularly strategic position. Joshua 2 tells how Joshua sent spies across the Jordan. Presumably these spies chose to lodge with Rahab because her house formed part of the town wall; it would have made a good observation post and they were well placed for a quick getaway. Probably for Rahab the location was good for her trade as well.

When Rahab is faced with the King of Jericho's demand to hand over the two men, she, like Tamar, acts out of self-interest. Knowing that Jericho will not stand against God's people, she hides the spies, lies to the king, and obtains a promise that when the invasion comes she and her family will be well treated. But as with Tamar, so with Rahab: what is good for her turns out to serve God's purpose as well. Thanks to Rahab, the spies return to Joshua unharmed, with first-hand information about the state of mind of the local population: 'Truly the Lord has given all the land into our hands; moreover, all the inhabitants of the land melt in fear before us' (Joshua 2:24).

Like Tamar too, whom Judah cheated out of her third husband, and whose second husband refused her marital relations, Rahab has suffered from ill-treatment by the opposite sex. Both women lack security. It is not unreasonable to assume that Rahab was poor, hence her prostitution, and that she may have longed for the social change which the foreign spies represent. But whereas Tamar's lapse from virtue was to act as a prostitute on just one occasion, for a specific purpose, Rahab was a full-time harlot. She can hardly be called excellent. By comparison, though, her devious tactic in sending the king's men off on a wild goose chase seems to be more like a clever move than a further descent into wickedness. Rahab shows herself able to think on her feet and take into account all the likely benefits of her action. Even so, Calvin comments rather primly, 'As to the falsehood, we must admit that though it was done for a good purpose, it was not free from fault.'[4]

There is much more to the story of Rahab than her lie, which many would see as no more than changing sides with the threat of imminent conflict. As with Tamar, there is the social consideration of her own vulnerable situation; and her action does much more than save her own skin. Just as Tamar's action led to something much bigger – the continuing fruitfulness of the line of Jacob – so Rahab directly facilitates the Israelites' invasion of Canaan and reassures them of their chances of success. Rahab the prostitute, says the Epistle of James, was 'justified by works' (James 2:25), while the writer to the Hebrews sets her in the wider context in which we have already encountered Sarah:

> By faith the walls of Jericho fell after they had been encircled for seven days. By faith Rahab the prostitute did not perish with those who were disobedient, because she had received the spies in peace. (Hebrews 11: 30–1)

Tamar and Rahab are linked in history by their life-saving, though arguably immoral, reactions in difficult circumstances. And there is another connection between them – a scarlet thread. In Tamar's case, a midwife uses the thread as a way of distinguishing the first-born twin. In fact the baby marked in this way was overtaken by his brother

(Genesis 38:28–30), so the thread comes to symbolize a certain rivalry between them. But we may see in it too the justification of Tamar's action, a symbol of her escape from a perilous (and childless) condition. This is certainly so of Rahab, who puts a scarlet cord in her window as a sign of special protection when the Israelites storm Jericho (Joshua 2:18–21). Thus a 'scarlet' symbol which today might be recognized as standing for immoral behaviour here represents, in the mysterious purposes of God, nothing less than salvation.

Sinful Women and Jesus

A marked feature of the Gospels, particularly the Gospel of John, is Jesus' readiness not just to treat women with respect but also to place himself alongside women condemned by society for sexual sin. In befriending such women and refusing to sit in judgement on them, Jesus offers forgiveness and establishes that if they repent they are just as eligible for salvation as religious leaders, if not more so. Jesus makes this point in no uncertain terms to the chief priests and elders who had refused to heed John the Baptist's call to repent: 'Truly, I tell you, the tax-collectors and the prostitutes are going into the Kingdom of God ahead of you. For John came to you in the way of righteousness and you did not believe him, but the tax-collectors and prostitutes believed him; and even after you saw it, you did not change your minds and believe him' (Matthew 21:31–2). Sinful women are among those who are blessed because they are not among those who saw and yet did not believe.

Jesus' willingness to allow himself to be anointed by a woman who, in Luke's account, may have been a prostitute (Luke 7:37) is further evidence of his ready compassion for sinful women. (After all, life is never that simple, and a woman does not sin on her own.) Similarly, in the case of the woman of Samaria, her many husbands do not stop Jesus from allowing her to spread the gospel message (see Chapter 4).

The Woman Caught in Adultery (John 8:1–11)

This episode has long been recognized as not being part of the original text of the Gospel. It is found in only one of the earliest Greek manuscripts, and is often considered to be more similar in language and style to the synoptics, possibly Luke. But there is no suggestion that Jesus' encounter with the adulterous woman did not happen, and its inclusion in the Authorized Version has meant that it is widely known.

We know little of the woman in question and she speaks only once. There is no doubt about her guilt, and she finds herself surrounded by her judges as she waits for the punishment which would take her to the point of death. Stoning was the penalty for betrothed girls who had been found in an adulterous relationship (probably with a married man), as opposed to strangulation if the girl was already married. We cannot know whether this terrified girl saw in the Pharisees' conversation with Jesus a ray of hope or a cruel delay in the carrying out of her sentence. She stands there mute, with no hope of escape from the imposing religious leaders surrounding her, not to mention the crowds who were already there with Jesus. Her loneliness and shame must have been overwhelming.

The question the elders put to Jesus is designed to trap him. If he tells them not to stone the girl, he will be failing to uphold the law of Moses; but if he pronounces a death sentence, he will be in trouble with the Roman governor, since it is he and not the Jewish leaders who has the authority to carry out capital punishment. Jesus does not deign to answer them, but instead bends down and writes something in the dust. We are not told what it was and it would quickly have been obliterated. (I once heard a leading evangelist make the rather charming suggestion that Jesus drew a heart with the initials of a religious leader beside it – 'Rabbi X loves woman Y, true'.) When Jesus does eventually speak, his words must have had some connection with what he wrote: 'Let anyone among you who is without sin be the first to throw a stone at her' (8:7). And, surely to the woman's amazement, her accusers one by one melt away, starting with the most senior, and sharing something of her shame as they hear Jesus' words.

But for the woman her ordeal is still far from over. Jesus stands before her, with his crowds of followers in the background, a single authoritative figure. Eventually he addresses her directly for the first time: 'Has no one condemned you?' (8.10). Her reply is a respectful, 'No one, sir', maybe recognizing in Jesus a higher power than that of the Jewish leaders. Jesus does not downplay what she has done by dismissing her offence. Rather, he just refuses to condemn her, and holds out a lifeline – forgiveness is open to her, 'from now on do not sin again' (8:11).

This woman, then, is not represented as a penitent sinner, nor does Jesus make any explicit reference to forgiveness. Yet in this far from excellent woman there is a message of hope that goes beyond her particular circumstances: that God's judgement is not human judgement. And the possibility of forgiveness is always on offer, however incriminating the circumstances.

Discipline in the Early Church: Sapphira's Greed (Acts 5:1–11)

When Jesus saw a woman in danger of her life because of her wrongdoing, his compassion for her enabled him to make a point about the nature of divine judgement. When confronted with what might look like a lesser crime in the early church, though, the apostle Peter seems more inclined to make an example of the guilty parties.

In Acts 4 we are given some details of the lifestyle of the early church community: 'There was not a needy person among them, for as many as owned lands or houses sold them, and brought the proceeds of what was sold. They laid it at the apostles' feet, and it was distributed to each as any had need' (Acts 4:34–5). A striking example is given by Joseph, named Barnabas, who sold a field and handed over all the money to the apostles (4:36–7).

Acts 5, though, introduces a couple who failed to follow this fine example. There Ananias has also sold some property but 'with his wife's knowledge' held back some of the proceeds, giving only part of the money to the apostles. In fact, it is nowhere stated that it was obligatory for people to hand over everything to the community. Peter seems to be making this point when he confronts Ananias: 'While it remained unsold, did it not remain your own? And after it was sold, were not the proceeds at your disposal?' (Acts 5:4). Perhaps Ananias had simply pretended that what he had given was in fact the total sum. If this was disproportionate to the value of the property, this would explain Peter's instant realization of what was going on, though he may also have had other instinctive or supernatural awareness of wrongdoing. Peter's words, 'Why has Satan filled your heart to lie to the Holy Spirit? . . . You did not lie to us but to God' (5:3,4), have a devastating effect on Ananias and he falls down dead.

Then it is Sapphira's turn. Peter first gives her the option of telling the truth: 'Tell me whether you and your husband sold the land for such and such a price' (5:8). Her lie provokes Peter into making a similar charge against her: 'How is it that you have agreed together to put the Spirit of the Lord to the test?' (8:9), and at the news of her husband's death she too falls down dead. It is a lesson in equality, although Sapphira might more charitably have been seen as an accessory. Her loyalty to her husband, though, wins her no favours: Peter gives her the chance to redeem herself and she fails to take it.

It could also be argued that the couple do not appreciate the full significance of what they have done, which Peter calls a lie to the Holy Spirit. But no one in that community is likely to make that mistake again: each of the deaths causes 'great fear' to those nearby and eventually to the whole church. So it seems likely that the unhappy fate of the couple is intended to demonstrate more than a lesson in communal living. The message that comes over loud and clear from Peter's words has to do with the holiness of the church, the body of Christ on earth. A sin against the church is a sin against God himself and cannot attract anything other than the harshest punishment.

So once again a less than excellent woman (although one supposes her to have been hitherto steadfast in her faith) is used to convey a message of great importance, not just about conduct and discipline, but also about the very nature of the church of God itself.

Elizabeth Barton (1506–34): The Holy Maid of Kent

Dame Elizabeth Barton OSB, a Benedictine nun, has been described as one of the first victims of the English Reformation.[5] She began her working life as a serving girl at Cobb's Hall, near Aldington in Kent. Her prophetic powers first became evident when in 1525 she suffered a seven-month illness, during which she experienced trances and while unconscious spoke about events that would take place in the future. She also received a prophecy of her own healing from the Virgin Mary, if she went to the chapel at Court at Street, where there was a statue of Mary which had been the focus of devotion, and where she was to revive a cult of the Virgin. Elizabeth was healed not on her first visit, but on a subsequent one in the presence of 3,000 people. Meanwhile she was becoming famous, with her employer now treating her as a member of his own family and the Rector of Aldington taking a special interest in her. Elizabeth was examined by a commission set up by the Archbishop who gave her a favourable report. She was then received into the convent of St Sepulcre, near Canterbury, where she took her vows.

In the late 1520s, rumours began to circulate of Henry VIII's likely divorce from Catherine of Aragon. Elizabeth, who enjoyed the protection of the Archbishop's chaplain, persuaded him to give her an introduction to Cardinal Wolsey, through whom she eventually had an audience with the King himself. Elizabeth was prophesying disaster for the King and for the country if his marriage was annulled, and she told Henry that if he married Anne Boleyn his reign would come to an end in seven months. In a sense she was right, for seven months later Henry was excommunicated by the Pope and under ecclesiastical law was no longer entitled to receive the allegiance of his subjects. She was therefore not only accurate in her prophecy but also to some degree successful in her professed aim of 'encouraging the Pope and his representatives to resistance against the King's indiscipline as displeasing to God'.[6]

Between 1528 and 1533 Elizabeth enjoyed considerable freedom in both Kent and London, 'exploiting to their limits both the customary latitude given to inspired women and the confused state of English treason law'.[7] Anne Boleyn's coronation at Whitsun in 1533 did not silence Elizabeth and now she began to challenge the new Queen. But things had changed. Thomas Cranmer had been Archbishop of Canterbury since April and had presided at the new Queen's coronation. Cranmer of course exercised authority over Elizabeth, as her convent was in his diocese, and the King ordered him to take steps against her. Elizabeth crumpled under interrogation from Cranmer, Latimer and Cromwell, and confessed that 'she never had vision in all her life, but all that ever she said was feigned of her own imagination, only to satisfy the minds of them the which resorted unto her, and to obtain worldly praise'.[8]

After his enthronement in December 1533, Cranmer continued what was beginning to look like a personal vendetta against Elizabeth. One of his assistants preached a sermon against her, and the Archbishop used his first visitation of his diocese to hunt out her supporters. He also wrote his own satirical summary of her activities, which included a description of her as 'heretical'. The new parliamentary session in January 1534 passed the Act of Succession, which protected the Boleyn marriage, and in April of that year Elizabeth and five of her followers were executed without trial as traitors, having previously been condemned by Parliament. Two of those executed were Franciscans and were offered the opportunity to renounce the Pope, which they refused to do. Elizabeth's body was buried at Grey Friars and her head displayed on London Bridge.

Elizabeth Barton's career was far from ineffective. Her support of Catherine and her condemnation of Henry's remarriage had been influential and the rift with Rome was significantly deepened. Her execution silenced a voice that was troublesome to the King and gave Cranmer the excuse to purge his diocese of many of the clergy appointed by his predecessor Warham, who had supported Elizabeth. The question remains as to whether her confession was genuine. It had been extracted after her imprisonment and written for her by her judges. Whether it was hers, or had been concocted by Protestant adversaries, remains uncertain.

Elizabeth may have been less than excellent either in inventing her visions or making a false confession. Either way, her unwilling contribution to the rapidly growing movement towards Reformation remains a significant one.

Rifts in the Church: Selina, Countess of Huntingdon (1709–91)

In 1728 there was a marriage between Lady Selina Shirley and the ninth Earl of Huntingdon, whose ancestry can, I believe, be traced back to one of the more bizarre women prophets active in England in the 1640s.[9] Selina, although not then an overly pious girl, had prayed from childhood that she might marry into a 'serious' family.[10] Until her marriage she had restricted herself to good works, but under the influence of her new sister-in-law, Lady Margaret Hastings, she underwent a spiritual transformation which, coupled with a serious illness, quickly led to a dramatic conversion.

This was the time of John Wesley and the Evangelical Revival in England, and Selina's new-found enthusiasm began to verge on the fanatical. Her biographer observes: 'Some urged Lord Huntingdon to restrain her but although he did not entirely share her convictions, his regard for her was such that he did nothing to interfere with her religious views.'[11] Noting a certain godlessness in the society in which she moved, Selina's self-appointed mission was to bring the Revival to her own class, a work which increasingly obsessed her:

> She gathered in her drawing-room large numbers of the rich and aristocratic, not for cards or dancing, but to hear one of the great evangelical preachers like Whitefield.[12]

George Whitefield, who was the most gifted and forceful of preachers, would come to the Countess's town house twice a week. He succeeded in making conversions among the nobility, and G. W. Kirby has a nice story to tell of the effect of his preaching on them:

> Lord Chesterfield, a professed atheist but a lover of good oratory, was on one occasion so entranced by White-field's portrayal of a blind beggar tottering on the brink of a precipice, that he bounded from his seat, exclaiming 'Good God, he's gone!'[13]

Most of Selina's circle were Methodists, but politicians and leaders of all kinds came to her gatherings and 'even bishops were smuggled in and hidden behind curtains'.[14]

It seems clear that at this stage Selina was not intending to break with the Church of England, although her activities could hardly be seen as a contribution to church unity. She appears to have had a Protestant spirit which wanted, perhaps unrealistically, to embrace all traditions. In Wales she founded a college to train ministers who might serve as evangelical clergymen either in the Church of England or in some other Protestant church. She also founded a number of chapels or meeting houses, mainly in London and the South-East, which were places where those expelled from the Church of England as Dissenters could come and preach and where new converts could come to build up their faith. Those who joined these 'societies' were also encouraged to continue attending their own parish churches. One of the best known and most long-lasting chapels (financed in 1761 by selling her jewels and functioning at least until the middle of the twentieth century) was in Brighton, next to Selina's own house in North Street. One of the most controversial, founded in 1774, was Spa Fields Chapel in Clerkenwell, as this establishment had previously been 'a place of amusement'.

Selina herself exercised formidable power over her college and chapels, appointing and dismissing ministers and arranging services herself:

> Few of the Evangelicals failed to submit to her authority, but John Wesley never quite succumbed, and John Berridge preserved a power of standing up for himself which does him credit: 'You threaten me, madam, like a pope', he wrote, 'not like a mother in Israel'; and 'my instructions, you know, must come from the Lamb, not from the Lamb's wife, though she is a tight woman'.[15]

In 1781, Selina's chapels, which until then had been societies within the Church of England, became Dissenting chapels, as their members would no longer accept the authority of the established church. From then on they were known instead as the Countess of Huntingdon's Connexion, which had its own 'Fifteen Articles', revealing a strong biblical emphasis. This was also the beginning of the final split between the establishment and Wesleyanism. Although John Wesley himself had always hoped to remain within the Church of England, his 'ordinations' widened the gulf between them, and when he died in 1791 his seventy thousand followers in Britain and Ireland and a further sixty thousand in America soon became a separate denomination. Indeed, Methodists may well have reason to be grateful to Selina for precipitating the movement which culminated in the founding of their own church.

By the time of her death in 1791, Selina had outlived all her Revivalist heroes, including the Wesleys and Whitefield. Some forty years later her Connexion comprised around two hundred chapels and missions with about thirty-five thousand worshippers. She had been an

extremely forceful woman who used her money and aristo-
cratic connections to get what she wanted. While her
character and the movement she founded could probably
never have existed comfortably within the established
church of the time, and although her chapels were eventually absorbed into other church denominations or closed
down, it could be argued that her heart was in the right
place. She was someone who perhaps unwittingly advanced
the cause of women, and Elliott Binns judges her kindly:

> That one of the most active and influential leaders of
> the revival should have been a woman, and a woman
> of quality, was something that mere human foresight
> could never have anticipated, for women in the eigh-
> teenth century were expected to keep in the background
> and to submit to the guidance and control of their
> fathers and husbands.[16]

*   *   *

While there are many distinguished women who might
shrink from seeing themselves as successors to the women
of the Bible, and who would be uncomfortable with the
label 'excellent', there are probably relatively few who
would welcome being called 'less than excellent'. And it
certainly seems presumptuous to apply such a description to
anyone living. Because I do not wish unwittingly to hurt or
offend any woman still alive, or indeed anyone's immediate
descendants, I have deliberately drawn the line over two
hundred years ago. This is not to underestimate the valuable
contribution of women whose flaws, great and small, have
been revealed in the cruel light of history. Like so many, perhaps the majority of Christian women down to the present
time, they too have been excellent in their way.

Women Giving Life

> Because women give birth and raise children with the
> experience of pain, long-suffering and heavy work, they
> have a strong sense of the preciousness of life and an
> attachment to life in general, not only for themselves
> but for others too.[1]

Giving or preserving life is an integral part of women's
culture and one which is highlighted at key moments
in both the Old and New Testaments. It is seen most
clearly in the great birth narratives, notably those of Elizabeth and Mary in the Gospels. But the female instinct to
preserve life by protecting vulnerable beings is not restricted to the birth mother, as examples from Exodus will
illustrate.

The anonymous Asian Christians quoted above also
comment that this life-preserving culture does not get
translated into a political and economic system within
human social structures. And it is remarkable that one of
the greatest stories of preserving life is a subversive one,
undermining the political structure of the time. Indeed,
Jesus himself is given life outside the framework of social
normality, and his early years are a story of life being
preserved in the face of political danger. In such situations, the role of the women who give and protect life is
central.

Shiphrah and Puah (Exodus 1)

It falls to two women who were possibly already old and certainly without any social status or privileges, to save the lives not just of an individual or small group, but of a whole race.

At the beginning of the Book of Exodus, the descendants of Israel in Egypt are marked by two things: their physical strength and their ever-increasing numbers: 'they multiplied and grew exceedingly strong; so that the land was filled with them' (1:7). Not surprisingly, the new Egyptian ruler sees this as a threat: in an unstable world, although presumably unarmed and powerless, the Hebrews could easily join forces with Egypt's enemies and use an Egyptian defeat as an opportunity to escape back to their homeland. So Pharaoh embarks on a programme of calculated cruelty and oppression, only to find that, despite their terrible lives, the people of Israel with their characteristic strength continue to thrive. The only solution that remains is genocide – a plan which will be imitated centuries later when another tyrant, Herod, orders the slaughter of Jewish boy children (Matthew 2:16).

But whereas King Herod would be able to use his military forces to do away with innocent children, the Pharaoh in Exodus 1 calls on two women. Trevor Dennis[2] suggests that these women could have been Egyptian, since the Hebrew is ambiguous ('Hebrew midwives' could mean either midwives who were Hebrew or who served the Hebrews, rather as 'French teacher' is ambiguous in English). Whatever their nationality, though, the impulse of Shiphrah and Puah to save life rather than destroy it, even though this puts their own lives in danger, is remarkable. And if they were indeed Egyptians, it is exemplary.

The women's disobedience may in fact be attributed to two things: their natural instinct to save children's lives, and their fear of God, which overrides any fear of Pharaoh that they may have felt. These two factors govern what they do, and they are soon summoned back to Pharaoh to explain themselves.

The midwives' response to Pharaoh is carefully formulated to appeal first to what he already knows about the Hebrews in general, that is, their unusual physical strength. They then introduce what Pharaoh cannot know, namely what happens when women give birth, suggesting that these strong women are always through with the birth before midwives can get to them. Dennis comments that this implies that the story must have originated with the midwives themselves, since men would never have seen a woman give birth.[3] Thus these women not only save the life of the Hebrew race by refusing to take part in genocide; they also ensure that the story of that deliverance is given a life of its own within the Exodus narrative.

That is not, of course, the end of the story. Pharaoh's command that the Hebrew children should be killed is then passed on to 'all the people' (1:22), not just to the two midwives. Even so, Shiphrah and Puah are rewarded by God who gives them 'families' (1:21). Probably this means that they acquire the social status of having their own households. But it is attractive to think that, if they were still of child-bearing age, this might have included having children of their own, a suitable reward for their life-saving actions.

Shiphrah and Puah could equally well be labelled women of courage. In their stand against Pharaoh (who might even have been their own national leader) they set an example to the Hebrews of fearlessness in a desperate situation. And they do this, not by departing from their normal lives and nature or by striking out into the unknown, but by quietly continuing their everyday work – to give life and to protect it, regardless of the danger to themselves. It is surely their commitment to life which gives them the courage and wit to respond so effectively to Pharaoh when the need arises.

Pharaoh's Daughter (Exodus 2:1–10)

The tale of two women (of uncertain nationality) saving the lives of many children, is followed straightaway by the story of one woman who protects the life of just one very important baby. And there is no doubt this time as to the unnamed woman's nationality: she is an Egyptian princess, the daughter of Pharaoh. With her, courage and the willingness to subvert social structures and disobey a tyrant is brought into the heart of the royal household. And there is another woman involved, Moses' sister, who, like the midwives, uses a certain guile to enable a life to be saved, as she arranges for the baby's own mother to come and nurse her son.

The episode of Moses' birth and his safe upbringing in the face of the Pharaoh's genocidal decree involves, then, at least three women as life-givers, or even more if we count the princess's attendants who keep her secret. First there is Moses' natural mother, who manages to conceal her son's existence until he has grown too big to hide any longer, whereupon she puts him in his basket on the river where he might have a better chance of survival. Then there is Moses' sister, who keeps a watch over the baby at a distance, and is well placed to intervene when he is discovered. She is so successful in this that she manages to get Moses restored to his mother, the original life-giver, to be nursed.

The third life-giver is Pharaoh's daughter. It takes only a little prompting for her pity to be translated into important action: she pays for the child to be looked after (although, ironically, this is hardly necessary since she is employing his own mother); she adopts him; and she gives him his name. There is further irony here in that the princess is taking the future leader of Israel into her own family, helping along the very process of the Hebrews' escape that her father was so anxious to prevent. And there is irony in Moses' name, which he is given to reflect his origins, '"because," she said, "I drew him out of the water"' (2: 10). But, as Dennis and others point out,[4] Moses will also draw his own people out – out of Pharoah's reach.

We are told nothing more about the Egyptian princess. Perhaps she was a rebel, deliberately undermining her father's authority; or perhaps she was responding to a young life in danger, just as the midwives did, but out of her natural feelings of compassion rather than because of her vocational background. Either way, history would go on to show her as having pointed the way towards life for a whole people by virtue of saving Moses, in direct contrast to the atmosphere of oppression and death which hung over the actions of her father and those he commanded.

Elizabeth and Mary (Luke 1–2)

The child in my womb leapt for joy. (Luke 1:44)

The stories of Elizabeth and Mary at the beginning of Luke's Gospel run side by side, and, as we have already seen in Chapter 6, they are also an echo of Hannah's experience. So close is the link between them all, that in some manuscripts of the Gospel Mary's song, the Magnificat (based on Hannah's song of rejoicing), is attributed to Elizabeth instead.[5]

The two annunciation scenes in Luke 1, however, differ from the promise to Hannah in several ways, not least because news of Elizabeth's baby is conveyed first to her husband. At first it looks as though Elizabeth's story is set to be just another fertility narrative. Yet here there is no importuning of God by the childless couple, although there is the suggestion that they have in the past prayed for a child (Luke 1:13). It is emphasized that Elizabeth and Zechariah have lived blameless lives (1:6), and clearly they are worthy parents of a significant biblical figure. What is most striking, though, is that in each appearance Gabriel gives first Zechariah and then Mary an idea of what their sons are to be. And already he is suggesting the unequal relationship between the two men: both will be great, but Mary's son will be the Son of the Most High. In each case the gift of life to the two mothers has Old Testament allusions: John will go before the Lord 'with the spirit and power of Elijah' (1:17); Jesus will have 'the throne of his ancestor David' (1:32). Putting this together with the detailed instructions as to John's upbringing, John's role as the forerunner is already very clear.

We are not told anything of Elizabeth's reaction to the news of her long-awaited pregnancy, although we do have Gabriel's wonderful words about her impending mother-hood: 'You will have joy and gladness' (1:14). Contrast this with the troubled state of Mary: for her there is not to be the incomprehensible but welcome gift of a baby late in life, but the still more puzzling and socially unacceptable event of a birth when she knew herself to be a virgin, and with, at that stage, no husband to protect her. Not surprisingly, her first reaction to Gabriel's news is one of perplexity. The contrast between the two women is further highlighted later on with Simeon's oblique statement to Mary that 'a sword will pierce your own soul too' (2:35).

The birth of John is a matter of great celebration; in the comfort of her own home, Elizabeth is surrounded by friends and relatives who 'rejoiced with her'. Mary gives birth in an outhouse; and the people who rejoice are shepherds (the outcasts of religious society) and angels.

Both women are to have sons who will die brutal deaths, yet there is still joy, even if in the case of the people who surround Mary it is inseparable from awe. For these two women, then, Mary, who accepted to become the most important life-giver of all time, and Elizabeth, who unexpectedly became pregnant with the forerunner of the Messiah, these key moments meant very different emotions.

In both cases husbands have an important role to play. Pregnancy could be seen as the result of Elizabeth's and Zechariah's life of faithfulness, which is unexpectedly rewarded. Their family history also played a part: both were descendants of Aaron, and male descendants were priests who had the privilege of officiating at Temple sacrifices. They were highly suitable parents for the forerunner. Mary's future husband, though, was descended from David, and, despite Joseph's initial hesitations, Matthew's Gospel calls him 'a righteous man' and he is immediately obedient to the angel's message to him (Matthew 1:20–25). His natural goodness is also apparent in his desire not to cause Mary public disgrace (1:19) even though he would at that stage have been well within his rights to do so.

As I have already suggested (page 94), it is the news of Elizabeth's pregnancy that provokes Mary's willing acceptance of Gabriel's charge to her (Luke 1:35–8). And it is this last detail which takes us into the next phase in Luke's narrative, as Mary goes straight off to see Elizabeth. On a human level, this is the very natural reaction of two women wanting to be together, not only because of their encounter with God but also to share their experience of pregnancy. Presumably Mary sought advice from her relative, but she herself would also have been a support to the older woman who, like Sarah, faced the demands of childbirth in later life. If they sought reassurance from each other about their sudden change in circumstances, this was at once given: the baby leapt 'for joy' in Elizabeth's womb, and Elizabeth's response to Mary echoes the words of the angel: 'Why am I so favoured, that the mother of my Lord should come to me?' (Luke 1:43, RSV).

Although the image of Mary and Elizabeth with their young sons has been a favourite one with great artists, there is no biblical evidence that the two women ever met again. Perhaps their later meetings, despite the considerable distance between them, was a family detail that was taken for granted and not one the evangelist felt it necessary to mention. In any event once John is born and named, Elizabeth disappears from the scene, in a kind of effacement before Mary which echoes her previous humility, and which prefigures the adult John giving way to Jesus: 'He must increase, but I must decrease' (John 3:30).

Mary's role as a giver of life, and her husband's as her protector, does not end with Jesus' birth. Their flight from Herod into Egypt (Matthew 2:13–16) is a telling reminder of Moses' escape from Pharaoh, thanks to his mother and Pharaoh's daughter. After that, though, Mary's relationship with her son has to be inferred from the few remaining episodes in the Gospels in which she figures.

Parental influence would necessarily have been a key factor in Jesus growing up to be strong and filled with wisdom, divine and human (Luke 3:40, 52), and the incident when Jesus gets left behind in Jerusalem listening to the teachers (Luke 2:41–50) reveals his parents' natural concern for him. Yet Mary would not have forgotten the extraordinary circumstances of her son's birth and she takes more care than most mothers in remembering and mulling over the events of Jesus' childhood.

Once Jesus begins his ministry, Mary's maternal role is almost at an end, though we glimpse her pride in her son at the Cana wedding (John 2:1–11), and may sense her hurt when Jesus reminds his followers that his true family is not a human domestic unit (Mark 3:34–5). It is only at the cross that Mary's belief in her son re-emerges and the bond between them is publicly acknowledged. The heart-breaking detail of Jesus' mother and best loved disciple remaining so close when all the other male disciples had fled, is only intensified when Jesus entrusts to each other the two people closest to him (John 19:26–7).

Yet Mary's lifegiving function may not yet be over. Many commentators see these verses from John as indicating that Mary is to be a founder member of the church, and this interpretation is strengthened by the reference in Acts to Mary being present in the upper room and praying with the disciples in the days leading up to Pentecost (Acts 1:14). So Mary is there giving part of the early breath of life to God's church on earth, her role as a life-giver thus coming to embrace the whole of the New Testament. In early church tradition she began to be referred to as the second Eve, following Paul's declaration that Jesus is the second Adam: 'For as all die in Adam, so all will be made alive in Christ' (1 Corinthians 15:22). Marina Warner comments: 'She is the second Eve, mother of all the living in a new, spiritual sense.'[6]

Nursing Back to Life: Florence Nightingale (1820–1910)

> The pioneers of one generation are forgotten when their work has passed into the accepted doctrine and practice of another.[7]

The sentimental attitudes towards her which beset Florence Nightingale in her own lifetime, and which have lingered on in the stories built up around 'The Lady of the Lamp' do her a great disservice. Florence was an outspoken critic of church and state, a woman of formidable courage and discipline, and above all thoroughly down to earth. In just a few years in the 1850s she transformed military hospitals and saved countless lives that would otherwise have been lost, not because of fatal wounds but because of poor hygiene. And in the years that followed her experience on the battlefields of the Crimea, she laid the foundations for modern nursing practice.

Opinions differ as to when Florence first sensed a call to work in hospitals. When she was seventeen she wrote: 'God spoke to me and called me to his service',[8] though one of her biographers claims that it was only in 1844 that she first knew her vocation lay with the sick in hospitals, and even then envisaged works of charity rather than nursing.[9] It has to be remembered that at that time nurses were notoriously immoral and hospitals were 'places of wretchedness, degradation and squalor . . . The sick came into hospital filthy and they remained filthy',[10] and Florence's well-to-do family was understandably appalled at what she wanted to do.

It was not until 1851, in the face of continuing family hostility, that Florence was able to get even a modicum of nursing training. She went to Kaiserwerth in Prussia, to a school run by a Protestant pastor and his wife, who had already established nursing orders (their graduates were called 'deaconesses') in England and America. This was followed by a short spell in Paris.

In August 1853, Florence became the unpaid superintendant of the Hospital for Invalid Gentlewomen, a small private hospital in London. It was a post which allowed her to develop her organizational and administrative skills. As a result of her success there she was invited by Sidney Herbert, an advocate of hospital reform, to lead a team of nurses to Turkey. So Florence took the first women, thirty-eight of them, to Scutari, where they were to care for British soldiers wounded in the Crimean War.

Florence was in Turkey for less than three years, but in that time, despite initial official hostility, she improved beyond recognition conditions in the military hospitals which were largely responsible for the high mortality rate among the wounded. When they arrived Florence and her nurses found the Barrack Hospital in an unspeakable state, and to make matters worse it was hit by a hurricane which destroyed all the stores. Undaunted, Florence had the hospital repaired and equipped, at least partly at her own expense, dug latrines and introduced proper hygiene procedures. She had a high view of her unenviable tasks, later writing to a friend, 'It is a religious act to clean out a gutter and to prevent cholera.'[11] She was not simply concerned for the medical wellbeing of her patients, but did her best to ensure that the wounded received sick pay.

If Florence was the pioneer of women nurses working behind battle lines, she was probably also their first casualty. She returned home with Crimean fever, possibly contracted during a visit to the battlefields, and remained an invalid for much of her life. It has also been suggested that she was suffering from post-traumatic stress disorder. Be that as it may, Florence came back a heroine, the public having been kept informed about the scandalous conditions at Scutari by the first war correspondents, who were using a novel piece of equipment, the telegraph. In 1860 she used money raised by a grateful public to set up a nurses' training school at St Thomas' Hospital in South London, and despite her frequent bouts of illness she remained involved and interested in hospital matters for the rest of her long life.

Florence did not shrink from controversy, not least as far as religion was concerned. Describing her as 'a religious visionary, rebel and radical', Rosemary Harthill reports her criticism of the Church of England and the 'lukewarm, hypocritical, unthinking religion of much of Victorian

England'.[12] She questioned traditional religious doctrine, claiming that the Ten Commandments were 'full of mistakes', yet she experienced visions she believed to come from God, and was drawn to the medieval mystics (some of whom, Cecil Woodham-Smith points out, were not bad administrators and organizers themselves), though she seems not to have approved of ecstatic experiences:

> The 'mystical' state is the essence of common sense ... the ecstatic state is unreal, and should not be at all ... we *can* only act and speak and think through Him.[13]

Nursing itself she saw as a spiritual vocation:

> Nursing is an Art; and if it is to be made an art, requires an exclusive devotion, as hard a preparation, as any painter's or sculptor's work; for what is the having to do with dead canvas or cold marble compared with having to do with the living body – the temple of God's spirit.[14]

She was firmly set against using prayer as a wish list:

> It did strike me as odd, sometimes, that we should pray to be delivered 'from plague, pestilence, and famine', when all the common sewers ran into the Thames, and fevers haunted undrained land, and the districts which cholera would visit could be pointed out. I thought that cholera came that we might remove these causes, not pray that God would remove the cholera.
>
> I gave up praying, in the sense of *asking*, from experience, and not from theory.[15]

She tackled the question of evil in much the same way, arguing that infection is a way of encouraging people to social improvement:

The lesson of 'infection' is to remove the conditions of dirt, of over-crowding, of foulness of every kind under which men live . . .

Disease is Elijah's earthquake, which forces us to attend, to listen to the 'still small voice'. May we not therefore say that 'infection' (facts and doctrine) shows God to be a God of love?[16]

Florence was back in the public eye in 1897, the year of Queen Victoria's Diamond Jubilee. An exhibition on the Victorian era had a section on the progress of nursing which focused on her work. When asked for 'relics and representations' of the Crimean War, she responded rather testily:

What are they? They are first the tremendous lessons we have had to learn from its tremendous blunders and ignorances. And next they are Trained Nurses and the progress of Hygiene. These are the 'representations' of the Crimean War.[17]

She continued to be courted and visited by the famous, including in 1898 the Aga Khan, whom she described as 'a most interesting man' adding 'but you never could teach him sanitation'.[18]

By then, though, her sight (for many years a problem) was failing fast as were her mental capacities. In 1907 she became the first woman to receive the Order of Merit, although she probably did not understand what was going on. Yet she lingered for another three years, blind and increasingly unable to speak, before her death in 1910. In deference to her wishes, her family declined to have her buried in Westminster Abbey, but took her home to the family grave.

Although Florence Nightingale's experience of practical

nursing was fairly short-lived, she was always interested in the intellectual and theoretical side of it. The reforms she introduced changed the face of hospital care, and have continued to save countless lives ever since.

Caring for the Sick and Dying: Dr Sheila Cassidy

Sheila Cassidy's name hit the headlines in 1975 when she was working as a medical doctor in Santiago, Chile. She had been called out to a young man – a revolutionary – who had been shot in the leg. Her penalty for treating him was arrest and imprisonment by the ruling military Junta and on three occasions she was subjected to torture by electric shock to get her to reveal the whereabouts of the revolutionary and his associates. Dr Cassidy herself had no involvement in politics. Yet as she says at the beginning of the book which describes her experiences in Chile, 'One half of the world sees me as a machine-gun toting revolutionary and the other half as a cross between Florence Nightingale and Joan of Arc.'[19] The latter description does not seem wholly inaccurate, for she seems to have had the life-giving talents and the courage of both these women.

Sheila had decided to be a doctor when she was fifteen, although even while she was still as school she was wondering whether she had a calling to be a nun, an idea which was to return a number of times in the years ahead. However, she went to medical school, first at the University of Sydney and then at Oxford, where she qualified in 1963. She thought her future might lie in plastic surgery: 'I had always been attracted by the challenge of rebuilding the broken and the burned, and visualized my future working in facial reconstruction and in hand surgery.'[20] First, though, she worked in Leicester as a senior casualty officer, and then in 1971 decided to go to a developing country for a couple of years' operative experience before returning to do plastic surgery. Her choice of Chile was down to her friendship with a Chilean doctor who had returned to Santiago to work in the city's poorest, dirtiest hospital treating the *rotos* (the 'broken ones').

Within a couple of years Sheila had obtained a Chilean medical qualification. But two things happened which were to influence the course of her life. In September 1973, after a military coup, the Junta took over and Chile became divided, caught up in an atmosphere of hatred. Then her friend Consuelo died of liver failure: 'Sad and lonely I sought refuge at the feet of God to whom I had given little thought for many years.'[21]

Returning to Chile in January 1975 after visiting her dying father in England and his subsequent death, she found the country in a state of siege. She went to work in the same hospital where Consuelo had been, and which she describes as 'one of the busiest and most ill equipped hospitals in the city'. She continues: 'It was in an area famous for its prostitutes and alcoholics and I came to practise a medicine very different from that which I had learned at the Radcliffe Infirmary in Oxford.'[22] But it was in the slums of Santiago that she came closest to God:

> It was easy to see the image of God in the sun setting behind the Andes ... but the image of Christ in his creatures is a very tarnished one and it is too easy to miss it ... I came to see him more and more in the broken ones of Santiago.[23]

Next, Sheila accepted the bishop's invitation to work in a new clinic in the shanty town of El Salto, which had been set up by El Comite pro Paz a year or so earlier. But now the Catholic Church was committed to denouncing the atrocities which were taking place across South America under dictatorial regimes, and El Comite was disbanded on General Pinochet's orders at the end of 1975. Cassidy writes of this period and subsequently: 'The Church of Chile, far from being the opium of the people, continues to fulfil its prophetic role and, refusing to be silenced, is the voice for those who have no voice.'[24] She goes on to add: 'Feeling myself unequipped for the work of changing society, I left it to others and tried only to heal the sick and comfort the desolate ... may God forgive me.'[25] Nonetheless she became increasingly involved with the hungry as well as the sick, and it was when she treated the young revolutionary Nelson Gutiérrez that she finally fell foul of the regime herself.

Sheila was captured on the night of 31 October 1975 and her captors at once subjected her to electric shocks in the hope of finding out where Nelson was and who was protecting him. After three sessions of torture she gave in: 'I remember little except that I prayed for strength to withstand the pain and for courage to die with dignity if that was to be my fate. Most of all I remember a curious feeling of sharing in Christ's passion.'[26]

Despite all this and a period of solitary confinement followed by a longer spell in a women's prison she did not condemn her captors. She writes, 'We mourned for our torturers and the men who found the torture justifiable'[27] and reflects that there must be many who were distressed by having to inflict pain. Nor did she lose her love for Chile. When eventually she was flown to freedom, she looked back at the country where 'war and peace, riches and destitution, hatred and love live side by side, and where paradoxically, in losing my life I had found it again'.[28]

. Some years later, back in the UK, Sheila Cassidy went into the field of palliative medicine, caring for the terminally ill and dying in hospitals and hospices. In a book on this subject she looks back to her three weeks of torture, describing them as 'a time of naked encounter with God'.

So she comes to understand Jesus' words in the Beatitudes, 'Blessed are the sorrowful':

> Those who mourn struggle with God until daybreak. Then, having seen God face to face and survived, they emerge wounded but knowing deep in their guts that he loves them, that all his world is holy ground and that death, when it comes, is quite simply the beginning, not the end.[29]

As a giver of life Sheila Cassidy suffered terribly herself, because she persisted in carrying out her medical tasks. She has built on that experience since, to give, like Mother Teresa, comfort to the dying and the hope of new life. For many people in Chile, though, she brought healing and restoration to life at a dark time in their history. In an article written in January 1976, and published as an epilogue to her first book, Bishop Jorge Hourton describes her farewell:

> Now she was waving the same hand that had touched so many sick bodies in our Policlinica of the Northern Zone, where so many had known and loved her – an open, honest hand, incapable of deceit or violence, as we all well knew.

And he pictures her plane taking off like a majestic bird: 'It seemed that it carried in its beak an immense olive branch.'[30]

Conclusion

Giving life is of course the ongoing calling of many, if not most women, whether they fulfil this as mothers or as carers. And women will continue to excel in that role, although in the future we can expect there to be many new and different ways in which they may do this. Some of it will have to do with progress in science and medicine. Already there are outstanding women in such potentially life-giving fields as genetics and in research into the human brain. But other challenges are posed by struggles for survival which come in a much more immediate form. As much of the developing world is hit by the devastating spread of the HIV virus, women who may have been looking forward to a relatively peaceful old age are suddenly finding themselves caring alone for their orphaned grandchildren, often considerable numbers of them, as their own sons and daughters succumb to AIDS-related illnesses. They too are life-givers in overwhelmingly difficult circumstances.

The same is true of the other categories in which I have looked for women of excellence. So, for example, while in the future there may be fewer and fewer women living in traditional religious communities, women will continue to support each other and work together in the same way as their biblical models. Again a changing society offers different possibilities for ways of women being together. Groups of Christian women supporting each other in their faith and witness may do so by living and working together, but new technology now enables them to spread their networks wider and link up with other women or groups of women across the world. And as we have seen in the case of the *dalit* women in India, women continue to come together when they experience a common bond of oppression, whatever its cause may be.

In this book I have been looking for extraordinary women. But this is not to underestimate the countless numbers of women who would call themselves ordinary, yet who have been of inestimable worth to those among whom they have lived and worked. The value of the good wife or virtuous woman, idealized in Proverbs 31, may be above jewels, but let's not forget as well that '*many* women' have also done excellently.

Notes

Chapter 1: Women Speaking Out

1 W. Eichrodt, *Theology of the Old Testament*, vol. 1, SCM Press, London, 1961, p. 298.
2 D. Watson, *I Believe in the Church*, Hodder & Stoughton, London, 1978, p. 282.
3 D.N. Fewell, summarized in K.A. Larkin, *Ruth and Esther*, Sheffield Academic Press, 1996, p. 65.
4 *Ruth and Esther*, p. 67.
5 All page references are to Suzanne Noffke, OP (ed. and trans.), *Letters of St Catherine of Siena*, vol. 1, Medieval and Renaissance Texts and Studies, New York, 1988.
6 Lavinia Byrne, *Women at the Altar*, Mowbray, London 1994.
7 *Woman at the Altar*, p. 8.
8 *Women at the Altar*, p. 71.
9 *The Universe*, 16 January 2000.
10 Lavinia Byrne *The Hidden Voice,* SPCK, London, 1995, p. 7.
11 *The Hidden Voice*, p. 37.
12 *The Hidden Voice*, p. 60.
13 Lavinia Byrne, *The Journey is my Home*, Hodder & Stoughton, London, 2000.
14 Interview, *Church of England Newspaper*, 27 October 2000.

Chapter 2: Women Taking Action

1 Jean Anouilh, *The Lark*, trans. Christopher Fry, Methuen, London, 1955, Part II, pp. 69–70.
2 See Keith Thomas, *Religion and the Decline of Magic* (1971), Penguin Books, Harmondsworth 1973, p. 644.
3 *The Catholic Encyclopaedia*, vol. VIII (1910), on-line version 1999.

4 Marina Warner, *Joan of Arc*, Vintage, Harmondsworth 1981, p. 78.

5 *Joan of Arc*, p. 89.

6 Joanna Bogle, *Caroline Chisholm: The Emigrant's Friend*, Gracewing, Leominster, 1993, p. 25. All subsequent page references are to this biography.

7 From Caroline Chisholm, *Female Immigration Considered in a Brief Account of the Sydney Immigrants' Home,* London, 1842, quoted in Mary Hoaban, *Fifty One Pieces of Wedding Cake,* Kilmore, Australia, 1973, pp. 58–9.

8 From *Microsoft Encarta Encyclopedia* (on-line), 'Caroline Chisholm'.

9 Don Chisholm, Caroline's great great grandson, *Microsoft Encarta Encyclopedia*.

Chapter 3: Family Women

1 Gerhard von Rad, *Genesis*, SCM Press, London, 1961, p. 281.

2 *Genesis*, p. 297.

3 *Genesis*, p. 297.

4 Roy Hattersley, *Blood and Fire: William and Catherine Booth and their Salvation Army*, Little, Brown & Company, London, 1999, p. 100. All page references are to this work.

5 *The Tablet*, 16 September 2000.

6 J. R. H. Moorman, *A History of the Church in England*, A. & C. Black, London, 1953, p. 388.

7 Diary entry for July 1941, quoted in Patricia Cornwell, *Ruth: A Portrait – The Story of Ruth Bell Graham*, Hodder & Stoughton, London, 1998, p. 86. Page references in the text are to this biography.

8 Quoted in Billy Graham, *Just As I Am: The Autobiography of Billy Graham*, HarperCollins, London, 1997, p. 111.

9 *Just As I Am*, p. 702.

10 William Martin, *The Billy Graham Story*, Hutchinson, London, 1991, p. 127.

11 *Just As I Am*, p. 252.

12 *Just As I Am*, p. 243.

13 *The Billy Graham Story*, p. 599.

14 *Just As I Am*, p. 709.

15 *Just As I Am*, p. 711.

16 *Just As I Am*, p. 703.

Chapter 4: Vulnerable Women

1 Gerhard von Rad, *Genesis*, SCM Press, London, 1961, p. 322.
2 Carlo Maria-Martini, *David: Sinner and Believer*, St Paul Publications, Slough, 1990, p. 41.
3 Walther Eichrodt, *Theology of the Old Testament,* vol. 2, SCM Press, London, 1967, p. 323.
4 D. Jasper and S. Prickett (eds), *The Bible and Literature: A Reader*, Blackwell, Oxford, 1999, pp. 152–3.
5 John Marsh, *Saint John*, Penguin Books, Harmondsworth 1968, pp. 215–16.
6 *The Book of Margery Kempe* (trans. B. A. Windeatt), Penguin Classics, Harmondsworth 1985, p. 297. All page references in the text are to this edition.
7 Janet Wilson, 'Communities of Dissent: The Secular and Ecclesiastical Communities of Margery Kempe's *Book*', in Diane Watt (ed.), *Medieval Women in their Communities*, University of Wales Press, Cardiff, 1997, p. 160.
8 'Communities of Dissent', p. 177.
9 *The Dawn of Hope: A Memoir of Ravensbruck* (1998), Arcade Publishing, New York, 1999, p. 8. All page references in the text are to this edition.
10 Jean Lacouture, *De Gaulle Vol. 2, The Rebel 1945–1970*, Harvill, 1991, p. 78.

Chapter 5: Suffering Women

1 C. E. B. Cranfield, *The Gospel According to St Mark*, Cambridge Greek Testament Commentary, Cambridge University Press, 1959, p. 185.
2 Henrietta Leyser, *Medieval Women: A Social History of Women in England 450–1500,* Weidenfeld & Nicolson, London, 1995, p. 219.
3 *Revelations of Divine Love* (trans. Clifton Wolters), Penguin Books, 1966, pp. 63, 75. All subsequent page references in the text are to this edition.
4 Simone de Beauvoir, *Memoires d'une jeune fille rangee*, Gallimard, 1958.
5 *Seventy Letters*, translated and arranged by Richard Rees, Oxford University Press, London and New York, 1965, p. 11. All page references in the text are to this edition.

6 In Simone Weil, *Oeuvres* (ed. Florence de Lussy), Gallimard, Paris, 1999, pp. 693–716.

Chapter 6: *Women of Faith*

1 Elaine Storkey, *Mary's Story, Mary's Song*, Fount, London, 1993, p. 65.
2 The rules relating to purification after childbirth in Leviticus state: 'If she cannot afford a sheep she shall take two turtle-doves or two pigeons' (Leviticus 12:8).
3 G. B. Caird, *Saint Luke*, Penguin Books, Harmondsworth 1963, p. 114.
4 Roger Ellis, *The Tablet*, 11 March 2000.
5 Quoted in Aron Andersson, *Saint Bridget of Sweden*, Catholic Truth Society, London, 1980.
6 *Revelations and Prayers of St Bridget of Sweden: the 'Sermo Angelicus' or Angelic Discourse Concerning the Excellence of the Virgin Mary Revealed to the Saint, with Certain Prayers* (trans. Ernest Graf), Burns, Oates & Washbourne Ltd, London, 1928.
7 Prayer of Mother Teresa in Robert Van de Weyer (ed.), *The Fount Book of Prayer*, HarperCollins, London, 1993, p. 353.
8 Quoted in Kathryn Spink, *Mother Teresa*, HarperCollins, London, 1997, p. 255.
9 *Mother Teresa*, p. 6.
10 *Mother Teresa*, p. 22.
11 Biography by Navin Chawla, quoted in 'Seeker of Souls', *Time*, 15 September 1997.
12 *Mother Teresa*, p. 75.
13 *Mother Teresa*, p. 299.
14 Quoted in 'Seeker of Souls'.
15 *Mother Teresa*, pp. 226–227.
16 'Seeker of Souls'.
17 *Fount Book of Prayer*, p. 352.

Chapter 7: *Poets and Prophets*

1 See K. Kraft, 'Hildegard of Bingen' in K.M. Wilson (ed.), *Medieval Women Writers*, Manchester University Press, 1984, p. 109.
2 'O Vis Aeternitatis (O Eternal Vigour)' in M. Fox (ed.), *Hildegard of Bingen's Book of Divine Works with Letters and Songs*, Bear

& Company, Santa Fe, 1987, p. 384. All text references are to this edition.

3 *The Washington Post*, 30 March 1986, quoted in Fox, p. ix.

4 Quoted in E. Alvida Petroff, *Body and Soul: Essays on Medieval Women and Mysticism*, Oxford University Press, New York and Oxford, 1994, p. 12.

5 Rosemary Radford Ruether, *Women and Redemption: A Theological History*, SCM Press, London, 1998, p. 84.

6 Frances Thomas, *Christina Rossetti*, Virago Press, London, 1994, p. 37.

7 Letter to Caroline Gemmer, 4 February 1870, in Anthony H. Harrison (ed.), *The Letters of Christina Rossetti, Vol. 1: 1843 –1873*, University Press of Virginia, 1997, p. 340.

8 Quoted in *Christina Rossetti*, p. 219.

9 *Letters, Vol. 1*, p. 309.

10 *Letters, Vol. 1*, p. 400.

11 *Letters, Vol. 11*, p. 91.

12 *Letters, Vol. 11*, p. 113.

13 *Letters, Vol. 11*, p. 158.

14 *Letters, Vol. 11*, p. 196 (the poem is included in a letter to Gabriel).

15 Quoted in *Christina Rossetti*, p. 364.

16 *Christina Rossetti*, p. 383.

17 Quoted in Richard Symonds, *Far Above Rubies: The Women Uncommemorated by the Church of England*, Gracewing, Leominster, 1993, p. 136.

18 William M. Ramsay, *Four Modern Prophets*, John Knox Press, Atlanta, 1986.

19 *Women and Redemption*, p. 222.

20 *Four Modern Prophets*, p. 74.

21 *Four Modern Prophets*, p. 75.

22 Mary Tardiff, OP (ed.), *At Home in the World. The Letters of Thomas Merton and Rosemary Radford Ruether*, Orbis, New York, 1995, p. 19.

23 *Sexism and God-Talk*, quoted in *Four Modern Prophets*, p. 79.

24 *Women and Redemption*, p. 79.

25 *Women and Redemption*, p. 81.

26 *Women and Religion in America*, 3 vols, Harper & Row, New York, 1981–86.

27 *Women and Religion in America*, vol. 3, p. xvii.

28 *Women and Redemption*, p. 223.

29 *At Home in the World*, p. 25.
30 *At Home in the World*, p. 222.
31 Alfred T. Hennelly, SJ, *Liberation Theologies: The Global Pursuit of Justice*, Twenty-Third Publications, Mystic, CT, 1995, p. 55.

Chapter 8: Women Together

1 Otto Eissfeld is among those taking this view, arguing that Ruth was composed as late as the fourth century BC (*The Old Testament*, Blackwell, Oxford, 1965, p. 483).
2 Katrina Larkin, *Ruth and Esther*, Sheffield University Press, Sheffield, 1996, p. 56.
3 C. K. Barrett, *The Gospel According to Saint John*, second edn, SPCK, London, 1978, p. 395.
4 John Marsh, *Saint John*, Penguin Books, Harmondsworth 1968, p. 43.
5 Sister Agnes, *The Song of the Lark,* Triangle, London, 1994, pp. 7, 8.
6 Sister Agnes, *A Tide that Sings*, Triangle, London, 1988, p. 113.
7 *Song of the Lark*, p. 10.
8 *Song of the Lark*, p. 80.
9 *Song of the Lark*, pp. 45, 69.
10 *Song of the Lark,* p. 45.
11 *Song of the Lark*, p. 174.
12 *Song of the Lark*, p. 174.
13 *Song of the Lark*, p. 134.
14 I am indebted to the book edited by Bhagwan Das and James Massey, *Dalit Solidarity*, ISPCK, Delhi, 1995, for much of the information in this paragraph. See pp. 146, 167 and 169.
15 In Ursula King (ed.), *Feminist Theology from the Third World*, SPCK and Orbis Books, London and New York, 1994, p. 134.
16 *Feminist Theology*, pp. 135–6.
17 *Feminist Theology*, pp. 136–7
18 *Dalit Solidarity*, p. 172.
19 *Dalit Solidarity*, p. 214.

Chapter 9: Less than Excellent

1 Park Kyung-mi, 'Genealogy and Women', in *Women of Courage: Asian Women Reading the Bible* (ed. Asian Women's Resource Centre for Culture and Theology), Seoul, 1992, p. 12.

2 J. C. Fenton, *St Matthew*, Penguin Books, Harmondsworth 1963, pp. 37–8.

3 Gerhard von Rad, *Genesis*, SCM Press, London, 1961, 1972, p. 362.

4 Quoted in notes to the passage in Eyre & Spottiswood Study Bible, 1964, Revised Standard Version.

5 J. R. McKee, *Dame Elizabeth Barton OSB, the Holy Maid of Kent*, Burns, Oates & Washbourne Ltd, London, 1925, p. 32.

6 *Dame Elizabeth Barton*, p. 30.

7 Diarmaid MacCulloch, *Thomas Cranmer*, Yale University Press, New Haven and London, 1996, p. 103.

8 *Thomas Cranmer*, p. 105.

9 This is Lady Eleanor Davies, who foretold the deaths (accurately) of her first husband, Archbishop Laud, and Charles I, cast herself in the role of the prophet Daniel, and announced that the resurrection of the dead would take place in the year 1700. Her daughter Lucy married into the Hastings family, and as far as I can tell from the family history, Lucy was the grandmother of the ninth earl.

10 G. W. Kirby, *The Elect Lady*, Trustees of the Countess of Huntingdon's Connexion, 1972.

11 *The Elect Lady*, p. 17.

12 J. R. H. Moorman, *A History of the Church in England*, A. & C. Black, London, 1953, p. 306.

13 *The Elect Lady*, p. 26.

14 *A History of the Church in England*, p. 306.

15 *A History of the Church in England*, p. 308.

16 Elliott Binns, *The Early Evangelicals*, quoted in *The Elect Lady*, p. 68.

Chapter 10: Women Giving Life

1 *Women of Courage: Asian Women Reading the Bible* (ed. Asian Women's Resource Centre for Culture and Theology), Seoul, 1992, p. 132.

2 See Trevor Dennis, *Sarah Laughed: Women's Voices in the Old Testament*, SPCK, London, 1994, p. 90.

3 *Sarah Laughed*, p. 94.

4 *Sarah Laughed*, p. 102.

5 Marina Warner, *Alone of All Her Sex: The Myth and Cult of the Virgin Mary* (1976), Picador, 1985, p. 9.

6 *Alone of All Her Sex*, p. 59.
7 Edward Cook, *Florence Nightingale*, quoted on a Florence Nightingale website: www.dnai.com/~borneo/nightingale
8 Rosemary Harthill, *Florence Nightingale: Letters and Reflections*, Arthur James, Evesham, p. 15. Harthill says Florence always wanted to do nursing.
9 Cecil Woodham-Smith, *Florence Nightingale 1820–1910*, Constable, London, 1950, p. 55.
10 Woodham-Smith, *Florence Nightingale*, p. 57.
11 Harthill, *Florence Nightingale*, p. 30.
12 Harthill, *Florence Nightingale*, p. 13.
13 Quoted by Woodham-Smith, *Florence Nightingale*, p. 525.
14 Harthill, *Florence Nightingale*, p. 64.
15 Harthill, *Florence Nightingale*, pp. 136–7.
16 Harthill, *Florence Nightingale*, p. 61.
17 Woodham-Smith, *Florence Nightingale*, p. 588.
18 Woodham-Smith, *Florence Nightingale*, p. 587.
19 Sheila Cassidy, *Audacity to Believe*, Collins, London, 1977, p. 2.
20 *Audacity to Believe*, p. 39.
21 *Audacity to Believe,* p. 71.
22 *Audacity to Believe*, pp. 102–3.
23 *Audacity to Believe*, p. 109.
24 *Audacity to Believe*, p. 129.
25 *Audacity to Believe*, p. 136.
26 *Audacity to Believe*, p. 193.
27 *Audacity to Believe*, p. 265.
28 *Audacity to Believe*, p. 333.
29 Sheila Cassidy, *Light from the Dark Valley: Reflections on Suffering and the Care of the Dying,* Darton, Longman & Todd, London, 1994, p. 83.
30 *Audacity to Believe,* p. 334.

Index of Names